AF103873

The Celestial Beauty of Jannah

DR. MUHAMMAD SALAH

Transcribed and adapted from the lecture

"When The Gates of Jannah Open: Divine Promises for The Righteous"

Published by:

TERTIB PUBLISHING

Unit No. E-10-5, Jalan SS 15/4G, Subang Square,
47500 Subang Jaya, Selangor, Malaysia
+603-5612-2407 (office) / +6017-399-7411 (mobile)
info@tertib.press
www.tertib.press
@tertibpress (Facebook & Instagram)

Author	:	Dr. Muhammad Salah
Transcriber & Editor	:	Nadiah Aslam
Proofreader	:	Ilyana Elisa
		Hanis Husna Adzhar
Cover designer	:	Abdul Adzim Md Daim
Typesetter	:	Abdul Adzim Md Daim

THE CELESTIAL BEAUTY OF JANNAH

First Edition: December 2024

Perpustakaan Negara Malaysia

Cataloguing-in-Publication Data

A catalogue record for this book is available from the National Library of Malaysia

ISBN: 978-967-2844-40-2 (hardback)

Copyright © Dr. Muhammad Salah 2024

All rights reserved.
No part of this publication may be reproduced, distributed, or transmitted in any form or by any means, including photocopying, recording, or other electronic or mechanical methods, without the prior written permission of Tertib Publishing.
Printed in Malaysia.

Contents

Preface 1

Part 1: The Key to *Jannah* 4

Chapter 1: The Race Towards *Jannah* 5

Chapter 2: The Mercy of Allah 10

Chapter 3: The Creation of *Jannah* and *Jahannam* 21

Chapter 4: The Way We Should Live 26

Part 2: The Description of *Jannah* 33

Chapter 5: The Place No Eye Has Seen 34

Chapter 6: The Rivers of *Jannah* 40

Chapter 7: The Fragrance of *Jannah* 51

Chapter 8: The Gates of *Jannah* 55

Chapter 9: The Levels in *Jannah* 62

Chapter 10: The Last People to Enter *Jannah* 68

Chapter 11: The Two *Bisharah* 74

Chapter 12: The Light of *Jannah* 78
Chapter 13: The Delights of *Jannah* 83
Chapter 14: The Comfort of *Jannah* 88
Part 3: The Footsteps of the True Believers 96
Chapter 15: The One Who Grieved When Separated 97
Chapter 16: The One Who Truly Loved 101
Chapter 17: The One Who Was Always in Prostration 108
Part 4: Acts and Supplications for *Jannah* 112
Chapter 18: Praying the 12 Sunnah Prayers 113
Chapter 19: Repeating after the *Mu'adhdhin* 116
Chapter 20: *Du'a'* after the *Adhan* 122
Chapter 21: *Du'a'* after *Wuḍu'* 126
Chapter 22: *Du'a'* to Be Firm on the *Deen* 131
Chapter 23: *Du'a'* for *Jannah* 136
Ending Remarks 140
Arabic Glossary 144

Preface

Assalamu'alaikum, dear readers, brothers and sisters in Islam.

The story of writing this book and other books to follow started with my journey to different countries to give lectures on Islam. Once, an attendant of one of my lectures told me that he transcribed the lecture, printed it and made it available for reading. Many showed great interest in reading the printed lecture for the knowledge it had. Then the idea came about collecting my lectures and publishing them in books. In every country I have come to visit, a team has become responsible for transcribing my lectures on a certain topic and preparing them for publication.

And so, consequently, many lectures have been published, printed, and distributed including to Islamic centres. *Alḥamdulillāh*, these books have been attracting a wide base of Muslim audiences due to their knowledge and benefits. Since then, I have dedicated this effort to disseminating Islamic knowledge and making it accessible to all walks of life.

For this book series, what motivated me more to write this book particularly is the approach I have taken to its theme, that is *Jannah*—Paradise and *Naar*—Hell. Firstly, I am presenting this theme as a narrative about the people of Paradise and the people of Hell by engaging with the following questions: who are these people, what are their characteristics, what do they do to deserve either place and how would they feel experiencing either place?

Second, I have relied on authentic texts from the Qur'an and hadith in answering these questions. And so, the reader shall feel assured about the resources and their authenticities.

Additionally, I have included stories based on the hadiths, so the reader's attention remains anchored to the text as they move forward. They can also connect the different sub-headings as part of one whole closely knitted narrative.

Furthermore, I have also referred to real-life stories and questions I have received from people during my career as a family counsellor. And so, the reader can relate to their own life experiences as well.

Next, I will guide the reader step-by-step on how to find the way to Paradise and tread it according to the teachings of Allah (s.w.t.) and His Prophet (s.a.w.).

Most importantly, I have concluded the book with a few *duʿaʾs*—supplications that the Prophet (s.a.w.) has taught us. These *duʿaʾs* teach and help us what to ask of Allah in our pursuit of attaining Paradise and avoiding Hellfire.

May Allah make this book and the knowledge it contains beneficial for us all and a means of guidance towards His (s.w.t.) path. *Āmīn*.

Dr Muhammad Salah

PART 1

The Key to *Jannah*

CHAPTER 1

The Race Towards *Jannah*

Assalamu 'alaikum, dear brothers and sisters.

Inshā'Allāh, in this book, I will be talking about the most favourite topic of every believer, *Jannah*—the description of *Jannah* and the dwellers of *Jannah*. May Allah the Almighty make us among the residents of the eternal abode of bliss.

I would like to begin with an important verse from the Qur'an about our journey to enter heaven. Allah (s.w.t.) said in the Qur'an:

۞ وَسَارِعُوٓاْ إِلَىٰ مَغْفِرَةٍ مِّن رَّبِّكُمْ وَجَنَّةٍ عَرْضُهَا ٱلسَّمَٰوَٰتُ وَٱلْأَرْضُ أُعِدَّتْ لِلْمُتَّقِينَ ١٣٣

And hasten to forgiveness from your Lord and a garden [i.e., Paradise] as wide as the heavens and earth, prepared for the righteous

(Qur'an, Ali-'Imran, 3:133)

In the verse above, Allah (s.w.t.) tells us not only to work hard to enter heaven but as a matter of fact, He (s.w.t.) also informs us to be quick—to hasten, to race, to compete in His forgiveness to make it into heaven.

In order to make it into heaven, we have to first stop at a station which is the Station of *Maghfirah*—the Station of Forgiveness. Thus, we should be quick to seek forgiveness from Allah (s.w.t.).

Allah (s.w.t.) mentions something similar in another part of the Qur'an, in surah al-Ḥadid:

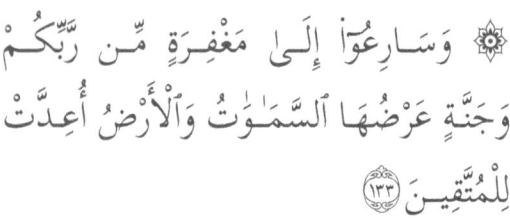

سَابِقُوٓاْ إِلَىٰ مَغْفِرَةٍ مِّن رَّبِّكُمْ وَجَنَّةٍ عَرْضُهَا كَعَرْضِ ٱلسَّمَآءِ وَٱلْأَرْضِ أُعِدَّتْ لِلَّذِينَ ءَامَنُواْ بِٱللَّهِ وَرُسُلِهِۦ ... ﴿٢١﴾

Race [i.e., compete] toward forgiveness from your Lord and a Garden whose width is like the width of the heavens and earth, prepared for those who believed in Allah and His messengers...

(Qur'an, al-Ḥadid, 57:21)

سَابِقُوٓاْ

Sābiqū

Race

Sābiqū means race. In the verse above, once again Allah (s.w.t.) is telling us to be quick and to race towards His forgiveness as a garden of eternal bliss which is as wide as the heavens and the earth altogether that has been prepared for them—for the ones who believe in Allah and His Messengers.

As you can see dear brothers and sisters, these two verses have some similarities. Let us observe them closer.

In surah Ali-'Imran, Allah says, "*a garden [i.e., Paradise] as wide as the heavens and earth, prepared for the righteous*"—meaning the eternal garden of bliss is extremely huge and spacious as it encompasses the heavens and the earth altogether, and it is prepared for the *muttaqin*, the believers. On the other hand, in surah al-Ḥadid, Allah says, "*a Garden whose width is like the width of the heavens and earth, prepared for those who believed in Allah and His messengers.*" As we can see, both verses mention that *Jannah*, the eternal garden of bliss is as wide as the heavens and the earth.

And so, both these verses have a few similarities. Firstly, about the divine guidance and the recommendation to work hard—to race and compete. Secondly, in order to make it into heaven, we must first and foremost obtain the forgiveness of Allah the Almighty.

Why must we work hard for *Jannah* and seek the forgiveness of Allah the Almighty? Because it is only through Allah's mercy that we will be able to step foot in *Jannah*. Even the greatest man to ever walk the earth—the Prophet Muḥammad (s.a.w.)—can only enter *Jannah* through the Almighty Allah's mercy.

Race toward
forgiveness from
your Lord.

Race toward a
garden whose
width is like
the width of the
heavens and earth.

CHAPTER 2

The Mercy of Allah

The Greatest Man to Ever Walk the Earth

In a sound hadith, the Prophet Muḥammad (s.a.w.) mentioned that, "None will get into Paradise unless they are showered with Allah's mercy:"

> "None amongst you can get into Paradise by virtue of his deeds alone." They said: "Allah's Messenger, not even you?" Thereupon he (s.a.w.) said: "Not even I, but that Allah should wrap me in His Grace and Mercy."
>
> (Ṣaḥiḥ Muslim 2816f)

None of us will be able to enter heaven simply with our righteous deeds.

We always tend to assume and think that we will be able to enter *Jannah* because we are very righteous and we have done a lot of good deeds. However, as we can see from the hadith, the Prophet (s.a.w.) mentioned that our good deeds alone—no matter how many they are—are insufficient to make any one of us eligible to enter *Jannah*, even the Prophet (s.a.w.) himself included.

As we all know, the Prophet Muḥammad (s.a.w.) was the greatest man to ever walk the earth. He was the final messenger of Allah (s.w.t.). He was the dearest and most beloved messenger of Allah (s.w.t.). However, he (s.a.w.) too can only enter heaven by Allah's mercy. The Prophet mentioned this in the hadith above. When the companions asked, "Even you O' Rasulullah?" He (s.a.w.) replies, "Even me. Unless the Almighty Allah showers me with His mercy." In essence, without Allah's mercy, without Allah's forgiveness, we will not be able to make it into heaven.

The Servant Who Worshipped for 500 Years

Dear brothers and sisters, I would like to tell the story of the *'abdi*—the servant of Allah who worshipped Allah (s.w.t.) for 500 years.

In the collected hadith, Jibril (a.s.) shared a story with the Prophet (s.a.w.) about the man who worshipped Allah (s.w.t.) for 500 years. The Prophet (s.a.w.) mentioned to his companions, "Jibril just visited me and told me about the servant from the nations before us who worshipped Allah the Almighty for 500 years."

On a side note, during that time it was the norm for people to live more than 500 years. As we all know, Prophet Nuh (a.s.) gave *da'wah* for 950 years but lived for over 1,000 years.

Back to the story, the *'abdi*—the servant—who worshipped Allah (s.w.t.) on top of a mountain all by himself for 500 consecutive years. He did not commit any sin. He was only worshipping Allah day and night. Allah the Almighty granted him a stream of water for him to drink and make ablution. He (s.w.t.) also produced food for the man to consume—a pomegranate tree which produced one fruit every day for him. And so, the man would eat and then continue in his worship to Allah the Almighty. The man later died in a state of worship—in the state of *sujud* as he had supplicated to Allah to allow him so. So, basically, the *'abdi* died in a state of worship and without any sins.

On the Day of Judgement, Allah will say to His angels, "Escort My servant to Paradise by My mercy." However, the servant will say, "O'Allah, rather grant me Paradise by my deed—*bi'amali.* I have worshipped you for 500 years and I did not commit any sins."

فَمَن يَعْمَلْ مِثْقَالَ ذَرَّةٍ خَيْرًا يَرَهُۥ ۝٧
وَمَن يَعْمَلْ مِثْقَالَ ذَرَّةٍ شَرًّا يَرَهُۥ ۝٨

So whoever does an atom's weight of good will see it, And whoever does an atom's weight of evil will see it.

(Qur'an, al-Zalzalah, 99:7-8)

فَأَمَّا مَن ثَقُلَتْ مَوَٰزِينُهُۥ ۝٦ فَهُوَ فِى
عِيشَةٍ رَّاضِيَةٍ ۝٧

> Then as for one whose scales are heavy [with good deeds], He will be in a pleasant life.
>
> (Qur'an, al-Qari'ah, 101: 6-7)

The servant will say, "Look at the scale of my good deeds. I have done enough to be eligible to enter heaven because of my good deeds." Allah will then say to him again, "Ya *'Abdi*, My servant, rather you will enter My *Jannah*, by My mercy." But the man will insist on allowing him to enter heaven through his deeds.

فَيَقُولُ لَهُ الرَّبُّ: أَدْخِلُوا عَبْدِي الْجَنَّةَ بِرَحْمَتِي

> The Lord says: "Enter My servant into Paradise by My mercy."

فَيَقُولُ: رَبِّ بَلْ بِعَمَلِي

> He says: "O' Lord, rather by My deeds."

Allah then calls His angels and commands them, "Weigh the 500 years of worship by My servant to the blessings that I have bestowed upon him." It is then revealed that the servant's deeds are not enough to even account for one of the blessings that was favoured upon him by Allah—the blessing of an eye, the blessing of sight, the blessing of being able to see. The deeds and the worship done by the man are not enough for that. On the scale, the man's worship is not enough to surpass the blessing of sight. The deeds and the worship are not enough to even give thanks and be grateful to Allah for one blessing—let alone His other countless blessings.

Allah's blessings are innumerable. It is said in the Qur'an as well:

وَإِن تَعُدُّوا۟ نِعْمَةَ ٱللَّهِ لَا تُحْصُوهَآ ۗ إِنَّ
ٱللَّهَ لَغَفُورٌ رَّحِيمٌ ﴿١٨﴾

And if you should count the favours of Allah, you could not enumerate them. Indeed, Allah is Forgiving and Merciful.

(Qur'an, an-Naḥl, 16:18)

If we were to count the blessings Allah has bestowed upon us, we would not be able to, we would not be able to keep the record of his countless blessings.

And so, Allah then says to the man, "Your worship is not enough for even one blessing." He (s.w.t.) will then tell the angels to bring the servant to *an-Naar*—to Hellfire. While being dragged to *an-Naar,* the servant will call out to Allah and say, "O'Allah, I would rather enter *Jannah* by Your mercy."

> "Enter My servant into Hell," and he will be dragged towards Hell, but he will call out: "O' Lord, by Your mercy, admit me to Paradise!" Then Allah will say: "Return him." He will be brought back and placed before Allah, who will ask: "O' My servant, who created you when you were nothing?" The servant will reply: "You, O' Lord." Allah will ask: "Was that by your doing or My mercy?" The servant will say: "By Your mercy." Allah will continue: "Who gave you strength to worship for 500 years?" The servant will respond: "You, O' Lord." Allah will ask: "Who placed you on a mountain in the middle of the ocean, provided you with fresh water from salty water, and brought you a pomegranate every night, even though it is typically only produced once a year? And who granted your request to die while prostrating?" The servant will say:

> "You, O' Lord." Then Allah will say: "It was by My mercy, and by My mercy, I admit you into Paradise. Enter My servant into Paradise, for you were indeed a good servant." Jibril then said: "O' Muḥammad, everything is by the mercy of Allah."
>
> (Al-Mustadrak, 7637)

This is a fact that we all must acknowledge: We will only enter *Jannah* through Allah's mercy, not by our deeds.

No matter how many good deeds we have done, it will never be sufficient. If I were to prostrate to Allah for the rest of my life, it would still not be enough to give my thanks and gratitude for even one blessing—what more of the other countless blessings. The same goes for you, dear brothers and sisters.

What are some of the blessings that we have received from Allah the Almighty? The blessing of being rightly guided to His path, the blessing of being chosen by Him (s.w.t) to worship Him alone and not associate Him with any other worship, the blessing of being able to speak, the blessing of being able to answer the call of nature without the need of assistance or someone to help carry us to the restroom and many more. The list goes on. We are unable to put a number to the blessings that He has given because they are countless.

In essence, we should bear in mind that we will enter *Jannah*—the place which Allah has prepared for the righteous believers—by Allah's mercy and forgiveness. That is why I mentioned the verses of surah Ali-ʿImran and surah al-Ḥadid in the first chapter, as we need His *maghfirah* as well to enter *Jannah*:

﴿... وَسَارِعُوٓاْ إِلَىٰ مَغۡفِرَةٖ ﴿١٣٣﴾

And hasten to forgiveness...

(Qur'an, Ali-ʿImran, 3:133)

سَابِقُوٓاْ إِلَىٰ مَغۡفِرَةٖ مِّن رَّبِّكُمۡ ... ﴿٢١﴾

Race [i.e., compete] toward forgiveness from your Lord...

(Qur'an, al-Ḥadid, 57:21)

Once Allah forgives us, once we are forgiven by Him, we will be eligible to enter *Jannah*, the place which is as wide as the heavens and the earth.

However, this does not mean that we should not do good deeds, dear brothers and sisters. We should strive to do good deeds and live in the way Allah has commanded to earn His pleasure and mercy.

Everything only occurs through the mercy of Allah the Almighty

CHAPTER 3

The Creation of *Jannah* and *Jahannam*

Al-Jannah wa an-Naar both exist, and the Prophet (s.a.w.) had seen both during his (s.a.w.) journey of *Isra'* and *Mi'raj*—when he ascended to heaven.

When Allah the Almighty created *al-Jannah wa an-Naar*, He (s.w.t.) sent Jibril (a.s.) to look at them. Allah said, "Jibril, pay a visit to Paradise. Have a look at the place and let Me know what you think of it." And so, Jibril visited *al-Jannah* and he saw what Allah had prepared for its dwellers. He (a.s.) returned to Allah (s.w.t.) and said, "I swear to Your Honour and Majesty that none shall hear of what has been prepared for its dwellers except that they shall make certain to enter it."

On the other hand, after Jibril (a.s.) visited Hellfire, he said, "I swear to Your Honour and Majesty that none shall hear about the punishment and torment of Hellfire but will definitely make certain to not enter it."

Afterwards, Allah (s.w.t.) made some modifications to both *Jannah* and *Jahannam*.

> "When Allah created Paradise and the Fire, He sent Jibril to Paradise, saying: 'Look at it and at what I have prepared in it for its inhabitants.'" He (s.a.w) said: "So he came to it and looked at it, and at what Allah had prepared in it. He (Jibril) said: 'Indeed, by Your Might, none shall hear of it except that he shall enter it.' Then He gave the order for it to be surrounded with hardships. He said: 'Return to it and look at it, and at what I have prepared in it for its inhabitants.'" He (s.a.w) said: "So he returned to it and found it surrounded with hardships. He returned to Him and said: 'Indeed, by Your Might, I fear that none shall enter it.' He (s.a.w) said: 'Go to the Fire and look at it and at what I have prepared in it for its inhabitants.' So he found it, one part of it riding the other. So he

> returned to Him and said: 'Indeed, by Your Might, none shall hear of it and then enter it.' So He gave the order for it to be surrounded with desires, then He said: 'Return to it.' so he (Jibril) returned to it, then he said: 'Indeed, by Your Might, I fear that none shall be saved from it except that he shall enter it.'"
>
> (Jamiʿ at-Tirmidhi 2560)

Allah (s.w.t.) surrounded *Jannah* with hardship and difficulty, such as the dos and don'ts—the halal and haram, obeying His commands and leaving that which has been prohibited. For instance, making sure to wake up for *Fajr* prayer every morning even though it is at a time that is earlier than our school time, work time or on weekends when we want to sleep in; or times when we are in the warmth and comfort of our beds and blankets. We give up all those comforts and strive to get up in order to pray as that is what Allah has commanded for us.

Is this something easy to do? No.

Do people like doing this? Only those who know that they have a meeting with Allah the Almighty.

In essence, *Jannah* is surrounded by hardships and

difficulties, which include abstaining from things that we desire and covet, giving up comfort, doing acts of worship, and more. *An-Naar* on the other hand, is surrounded with *ash-shahawat*—the things we desire—the things that we like and want.

And so, when Jibril (a.s.) visited *Jannah* and *Jahannam* after Allah made the modifications, he said, "I'm afraid that no one will make it into Paradise and I'm afraid that no one will skip Hellfire." Why did Jibril say, "No one will be able to skip hellfire?" Because it is very slippery. *An-Naar* is slippery as it is surrounded by pleasures—the prohibited actions and desires.

In a nutshell, all the desired things which are haram will lead us to the gates of *Jahannam*. Meanwhile, obeying all the commandments of the Almighty Allah and leaving His prohibitions will lead us to *Jannah*.

Let us be wise in our actions as they will determine which destination we will go to.

The journey to *Jannah* is surrounded by challenges and sacrifices but it is worth it.

Jannah is worth every single drop of our tears, every fall and every hardship.

CHAPTER 4

The Way We Should Live

As I mentioned in the previous chapter, *Jannah* is surrounded by hardship and challenges. And so, entering *Jannah* is not a piece of cake. It is not something that will happen by just saying the *shahadah*—by just saying, "I believe in Allah." We won't be eligible for *Jannah* with just the *shahadah* alone.

That is why, dear brothers and sisters if we read the Qur'an thoroughly, we will realise two things. Firstly, the number of times Allah has mentioned Paradise in the Qur'an, Allah has also mentioned alongside it the Hellfire as well. *Jannah* and *Jahannam*, reward and punishment—both are mentioned alongside each other to keep balance.

Secondly, in the Qur'an, not once does Allah

mention—in the verses about *Jannah* and its residents—that those who simply believe in Him will enter *Jannah*. Rather, in over sixty different verses, we find the phrase "*āmanū wa'amilūṣ-ṣāliḥāti*"—meaning those who believe and do righteous deeds.

We have to obey Allah and strive to do good deeds. I mentioned in the earlier chapters that we will not enter heaven with our deeds but with Allah's mercy. However, that does not mean we should not do any good deeds. Our good deeds are a sign of Allah's mercy and a sign of the believers working hard to please their Lord by living in the way He commanded.

إِنَّ ٱلَّذِينَ ءَامَنُوا۟ وَعَمِلُوا۟ ٱلصَّٰلِحَٰتِ
كَانَتْ لَهُمْ جَنَّٰتُ ٱلْفِرْدَوْسِ نُزُلًا ﴿١٠٧﴾
خَٰلِدِينَ فِيهَا لَا يَبْغُونَ عَنْهَا حِوَلًا ﴿١٠٨﴾

Indeed, those who have believed and done righteous deeds—they will have the Gardens of Paradise as a lodging, Wherein they abide eternally. They will not desire from it any transfer.

(Qur'an, al-Kahf, 18:107-108)

Indeed, those who believe in the existence and oneness of Allah, that He has no partners or counterparts and do good righteous deeds will be eligible to enter His *Jannah*.

However, as I mentioned, simply saying "*āmantu billah*"—I believe in the existence and oneness of Allah—alone is not enough.

Once, a sister brought her son to me and said, "My son doesn't pray, and he doesn't want to pray no matter how many times I advise him and try to convince him." And so, I spoke with her son, and I asked him why he was not praying when he was a Muslim. He said, "Shaykh, isn't there a hadith that says if our last words are '*Lā ʾilāha ʾillā-llāh*' we will enter *Jannah*?"

> The Messenger of Allah (s.a.w.) said, "He whose last words are: '*Lā ʾilāha ʾillā-llāh*' (There is no true god except Allah) will enter *Jannah*.'"
>
> (Riyaḍ aṣ-Ṣaliḥin 917)

I said, "Yes. That is a sound hadith." And then he said, "I am planning to say that before I die. So what is the purpose of praying if I already know how to enter *Jannah* without having to pray, fast and do all the other things." I said to him, "You wish. Do you really think Allah will let you say those words when you do not obey His commands?"

What does Allah say in the Qur'an my dear brothers and sisters? Allah the Almighty says:

يُثَبِّتُ ٱللَّهُ ٱلَّذِينَ ءَامَنُوا۟ بِٱلْقَوْلِ ٱلثَّابِتِ فِى ٱلْحَيَوٰةِ ٱلدُّنْيَا وَفِى ٱلْءَاخِرَةِ ۖ وَيُضِلُّ ٱللَّهُ ٱلظَّٰلِمِينَ ۚ وَيَفْعَلُ ٱللَّهُ مَا يَشَآءُ ٢٧

Allah keeps firm those who believe, with the firm word, in worldly life and in the Hereafter. And Allah sends astray the wrongdoers. And Allah does what He wills.

(Qur'an, Ibrahim, 14:27)

On the brink of death, whom will Allah keep firm? The believers who were steadfast in this life—the ones who were obedient to the Almighty Allah in this life. To those people, Allah will allow and inspire them to say the words, "*Lā ʾilāha ʾillā-llāh,*" as their last.

On the other hand, those people who lived their

lives in the opposite direction of what Allah has commanded; for instance, drinking, singing, clubbing and more, will die in that same fashion. If they lived by singing and indulging in music, they would be singing even when they were dying. We will die in the same fashion that we lived, and we will be resurrected in that state as well:

> Jabir reported: The Messenger of Allah (s.a.w.) said, "Every servant will be resurrected upon the way that they died."
>
> (Ṣaḥiḥ Muslim 2878)

One dies upon the path that he lived on and is resurrected according to what he died on.

When we die in the same fashion we lived, we will be resurrected in the same fashion as well. Meaning, *ḥusnul khatimah*—a good death—the good conclusion of life will determine the person's fate. Therefore, saying, "*Lā ʾilāha ʾillā-llāh,*" prior to death will indeed guarantee salvation and eligibility to *Jannah*. However, not everyone will be inspired to say those words. No. Only those who truly believed that Allah is their Lord and took action in obeying His commands and remaining steadfast in His straight path will:

إِنَّ ٱلَّذِينَ قَالُوا۟ رَبُّنَا ٱللَّهُ ثُمَّ ٱسْتَقَـٰمُوا۟ تَتَنَزَّلُ
عَلَيْهِمُ ٱلْمَلَـٰٓئِكَةُ أَلَّا تَخَافُوا۟ وَلَا تَحْزَنُوا۟
وَأَبْشِرُوا۟ بِٱلْجَنَّةِ ٱلَّتِى كُنتُمْ تُوعَدُونَ ﴿٣٠﴾

Indeed, those who have said, "Our Lord is Allah" and then remained on a right course—the angels will descend upon them, [saying, "Do not fear and do not grieve but receive good tidings of Paradise, which you were promised."

(Qur'an, Fuṣṣilat, 41:30)

The way we live will determine the way we die.

The way we die will determine the way we are resurrected.

Therefore, pay heed to the way we live as it determines our fate.

PART 2

The Description of *Jannah*

CHAPTER 5

The Place No Eye Has Seen

Narrated Abu Hurayrah:

> The Prophet (s.a.w.) said, "Allah said, 'I have prepared for My pious worshippers such things that no eye has ever seen, no ear has ever heard of, and nobody has ever thought of. All that is reserved, besides which, all that you have seen, is nothing.'" Then he recited: "No soul knows what is kept hidden (in reserve) for them of joy as a reward for what they used to do." (32.17)

(Ṣaḥiḥ al-Bukhari 4780)

Allah the Almighty says, "I have prepared for my righteous servants in heaven what no eye has ever seen, what no ear has ever heard and what has never crossed anybody's mind."

If our children were to ask, "Will we have PlayStation 7 in heaven?" Tell them yes. Anything we dream and wish for—all the food and drinks that we want, we will get them there, *inshā'Allāh*. Additionally, the foods that are mentioned in the Qur'an pertaining to *Jannah* are only similar to the *dunya* by its name but the likes and essence of it are completely different—it is the like of which no one has ever seen and tasted. It has never crossed anybody's mind. This is mentioned in the Qur'an and that is why the narrator of the hadith above, Abu Hurayrah (r.a.) quoted it:

فَلَا تَعْلَمُ نَفْسٌ مَّآ أُخْفِىَ لَهُم مِّن قُرَّةِ
أَعْيُنٍ جَزَآءًۢ بِمَا كَانُوا۟ يَعْمَلُونَ ﴿١٧﴾

And no soul knows what has been hidden for them of comfort for eyes [i.e., satisfaction] as reward for what they used to do.

(Qur'an, as-Sajdah, 32:17)

Allah has prepared for the dwellers of *Jannah* in the eternal abode of bliss, comfort for their eyes, and pleasure of love as a reward for what they did.

While reading this, some might be wondering about

the lines from the verse, "*Jannah* as a reward for what they used to do," because this means that our deeds will help us get into *Jannah*—which is a bit different than what I had mentioned in the earlier chapter.

In the earlier chapter, I mentioned the hadith that says, "None will simply enter heaven just by their good deeds." And so, some might be questioning why I am saying the opposite now. Some might be questioning how to reconcile these two opposite matters that I have mentioned.

Do not worry dear brothers and sisters, it is very simple actually to explain and reconcile these two hadiths. However, before that, I would like to ask you a question and I would like you to ponder on it.

Who woke you up for the *Fajr* prayer today? Please do not say it was because of the alarm because it was not.

It was Allah (s.w.t.) who woke us up. Allah invited us to pray because He loves us. Had it not been for Allah who guided us and made us love the prayer, the *ḥijab* and made us hate alcohol, drinking, dancing and all the *fawaḥish*—we would have been in despair and astray from the straight path.

Whomsoever Allah guides is truly the guided one, and whomsoever Allah leaves astray none can show him guidance. In essence, when Allah guides us to do good and righteous deeds, it is His blessing, it is His *raḥmah*. Hence, we have to be grateful to Him (s.w.t.) for this magnificent blessing as well.

Back to the hadith and the verse from surah as-Sajdah. If somebody were to ask us, "How does *Jannah* look like?" or, "What kind of joy and delight will we get in *Jannah*?" The above hadith and verse from surah as-Sajdah are one of the most beautiful, simplest and briefest answers we can give.

Some people might ask, "What is something that will make us want *Jannah*?" To this question, saying, "We will meet Allah, and we will meet His beloved Messenger Muḥammad (s.a.w.)," is a beautiful answer as well. Is it not sufficient, dear readers, to meet Allah the Almighty? It is more than sufficient.

Do you recall the supplication made by Asiyah bint Muzaḥim?

What was the supplication made by Asiyah (r.a.), the wife of Firʿawn? What did she say? She said:

... رَبِّ ٱبْنِ لِى عِندَكَ بَيْتًا فِى ٱلْجَنَّةِ ... ﴿١١﴾

..."My Lord, build for me near You a house in Paradise..."

(Qur'an, at-Taḥrim, 66:11)

Asiyah (r.a.) did not just make *du'a'* for a house to be built in *Jannah* for her, but she said she wanted near Allah (s.w.t.) a house built in *Jannah*. She supplicated to be near Allah—she wanted to be with Allah. And so do keep this important matter in mind.

Being able to see Allah in *Jannah*, being able to be with the Prophet Muḥammad (s.a.w.) and his righteous companions in *Jannah*, is something that is sufficient for us to want *Jannah*.

Jannah is a place where no eye has ever seen, no ear has ever heard and no mind has ever imagined

CHAPTER 6

The Rivers of *Jannah*

Ḥawḍ al-Kawthar

Before I delve into the four rivers of *Jannah*, I would first like to touch upon the water we will drink from, *inshā'Allāh,* on the Day of Judgement as it is related to one of the rivers of *Jannah*.

On the Day of Judgement, we will seek intercession. The order will be that we will first go to Prophet Adam (a.s.), then to Nuḥ (a.s.), then to Ibrahim (a.s.) in seeking *shafa'ah*—intercession. However, they will all decline, and we would be then referred to the Prophet Muḥammad (s.a.w.) and he (s.a.w.) will then rise by the will of Allah and intercede to begin the reckoning.

Additionally, on the Day of Judgement, we will all be extremely thirsty as well. And so, something will appear, which is *al-Ḥawḍ*. What is *al-Ḥawḍ* dear brothers and sisters? Many get confused with *al-Ḥawḍ* and *al-Kawthar*. Some even think they are the same thing, but they are not.

Ḥawḍ al-Kawthar is the Pond of Abundance, also known as the Pond of *al-Kawthar.*

What did the Prophet (s.a.w.) say about *al-Ḥawḍ*? He (s.a.w.) mentioned, "Allah bestowed upon me the blessing of giving me *al-Ḥawḍ*—a huge basin, a huge pond on the Day of Judgement. Whoever takes a sip from it will never get thirsty afterwards. The water is sweeter than honey, whiter than milk and its fragrance is better than the musk itself."

Narrated ʿAbdullah bin ʿAmr:

> The Prophet (s.a.w.) said, "My Lake-Fount is (so large that it takes) a month's journey to cross it. Its water is whiter than milk, and its smell is nicer than musk (a kind of Perfume), and its drinking cups are (as numerous) as the (number of) stars of the sky; and whoever drinks from it, will never be thirsty."

(Ṣaḥiḥ al-Bukhari 6579)

In the Qur'an, the shortest surah is al-Kawthar and it is mentioned in the surah that the river of *al-Kawthar* has been promised to the Prophet Muḥammad (s.a.w.):

إِنَّآ أَعْطَيْنَـٰكَ ٱلْكَوْثَرَ ﴿١﴾ فَصَلِّ لِرَبِّكَ وَٱنْحَرْ ﴿٢﴾ إِنَّ شَانِئَكَ هُوَ ٱلْأَبْتَرُ ﴿٣﴾

Indeed, We have granted you, [O' Muḥammad], *al-Kawthar*. So pray to your Lord and offer sacrifice [to Him alone]. Indeed, your enemy is the one cut off.

(Qur'an, al-Kawthar, 108:1-3)

Back to the question: What is the difference between *al-Ḥawḍ* and *al-Kawthar*?

First, we must keep in mind that these two are different things—different entities. *Al-Ḥawḍ* is a huge pond. The Prophet (s.a.w.) mentioned in the above hadith that the length of *al-Ḥawḍ* can cover the travelled distance of a whole month. He (s.a.w.) also mentioned that the pond is surrounded by vessels that outnumber the stars and planets. It is a humongous pond, and whoever takes a sip from it, their thirst will be quenched forever.

Ḥawḍ al-Kawthar, the pond of *al-Kawthar* is not in *Jannah*. It is before we even cross the *ṣiraṭ*. It is on the Day of Judgement. It is on the Day of Reckoning when all the believers will be thirsty.

Where does the water from the *al-Ḥawḍ*—lake—come from? It is from the river of *al-Kawthar*. This river originates from *Jannatul-Firdaws*—beneath the *'Arsh*, the throne of the Almighty Allah.

In essence, the water from *Ḥawḍ al-Kawthar* is coming from the river of *al-Kawthar*. We will see the lake, *Ḥawḍ al-Kawthar* on the Day of Judgement, and we will see the river of *al-Kawthar* when we enter *Jannah inshā'Allāh*.

And so, *al-Ḥawḍ* is before we enter *Jannah*. That is why it is mentioned in the hadiths that some of the *ummah* will be pushed away from *al-Ḥawḍ*:

ʿAbdullah ibn ʿAmr al-ʿAs, reported Allah's Messenger (s.a.w.) as saying:

> My Cistern (is so wide and broad that it requires) a month's journey (to go round it) all, and its sides are equal and its water is whiter than silver, and its odour is more fragrant than the fragrance of musk, and its jugs (placed around it) are like stars in the sky; and he who

would drink from it would never feel thirsty after that. Asma', daughter of Abu Bakr said: Allah's Messenger (s.a.w.) said: "I would be on the Cistern so that I would be seeing those who would be coming to me from you, but some people would be detained (before reaching me). I would say: My Lord, they are my followers and belong to my *ummah*, and it would be said to me: Do you know what they did after you? By Allah, they did not do good after you, and they turned back upon their heels." He (the narrator) said: Ibn Abu Mulaykah used to say (in supplication): O' Allah, I seek refuge with Thee that we should turn back upon our heels or put to any trial about our religion.

(Ṣaḥiḥ Muslim 2292, 2293)

On the Day of Judgement, there will be believers who want to drink from *al-Ḥawḍ* but they would not be able to. They will be standing near the lake of *al-Kawthar*, but they cannot come close to it. Upon seeing this, the Prophet (s.a.w.) will then ask Allah, "O' Allah Almighty, they are my people, my companions and my *ummah*. Why are they not allowed to drink?" Allah will then say, "You have no idea what they have done after you. These people have cursed the companions. These people have changed the religion and have created many innovations in the *deen*." Upon hearing that, the Prophet (s.a.w.) will say, "*Suḥqan, suḥqan*—keep them away, keep them away."

Sahl bin Saʿd reported:

> I heard Allah's Apostle (s.a.w.) as saying: I shall go to the Cistern before you and he who comes would drink and he who drinks would never feel thirsty, and there would come to me people whom I would know and who would know me. Then there would be intervention between me and them. Abu Ḥazim said that Nuʿman bin Abu ʿAyyash heard it and I narrated to them this hadith, and said: Is it this that you heard Sahl saying? He said: Yes, and I bear witness to the fact that I heard it from Abu Saʿid Khudri also, but he made this addition that he (the Holy Prophet) would say: They are my followers, and it would be said to him: You do not know what they did after you and I will say to them: Woe to him who changes (his religion) after me.

(Ṣaḥiḥ Muslim 2290, 2291a)

And so, on the Day of Judgement, the people who created innovations upon the *deen* will be kept away from *al-Ḥawḍ*. However, when we enter *Jannah*, there will be no restrictions. *Al-Ḥawḍ* is different, as it is before *Jannah*—it is on the Day of Judgement.

لَهُم مَّا يَشَآءُونَ فِيهَا وَلَدَيْنَا مَزِيدٌ ۝٣٥

They will have whatever they wish therein, and with Us is more.

(Qur'an, Qaf, 50:35)

Nothing is forbidden in *Jannah*. Nothing is restricted in *Jannah*.

Anything we dream of, anything we desire, we will get it, *inshā'Allāh*, when we step foot in the eternal abode of bliss. There is no haram nor restrictions in *Jannah*. Nothing is prevented. And so that is why *al-Ḥawḍ* has restriction because it is not in *Jannah*, it is before *Jannah*—on the Day of Judgement. In a nutshell, that is the difference between *Ḥawḍ al-Kawthar* and the river of *al-Kawthar*.

The Four Rivers of *Jannah*

It is mentioned in the Qur'an that one of the descriptions of *Jannah* is that it will have four rivers—the river of pure water, the river of milk, the river of honey and the river of wine, and its taste never changes, it is unaltered. This is mentioned in surah Muḥammad:

مَّثَلُ ٱلْجَنَّةِ ٱلَّتِى وُعِدَ ٱلْمُتَّقُونَ ۖ فِيهَآ
أَنْهَٰرٌ مِّن مَّآءٍ غَيْرِ ءَاسِنٍ وَأَنْهَٰرٌ مِّن لَّبَنٍ
لَّمْ يَتَغَيَّرْ طَعْمُهُۥ وَأَنْهَٰرٌ مِّنْ خَمْرٍ لَّذَّةٍ
لِّلشَّٰرِبِينَ وَأَنْهَٰرٌ مِّنْ عَسَلٍ مُّصَفًّى ۖ وَلَهُمْ
فِيهَا مِن كُلِّ ٱلثَّمَرَٰتِ وَمَغْفِرَةٌ مِّن رَّبِّهِمْ
ۖ كَمَنْ هُوَ خَٰلِدٌ فِى ٱلنَّارِ وَسُقُوا۟ مَآءً
حَمِيمًا فَقَطَّعَ أَمْعَآءَهُمْ ﴿١٥﴾

Is the description of Paradise, which the righteous are promised, wherein are rivers of water unaltered, rivers of milk the taste of which never changes, rivers of wine delicious

> to those who drink, and rivers of purified honey, in which they will have from all [kinds of] fruits and forgiveness from their Lord... [Are its inhabitants] like those who abide eternally in the Fire and are given to drink scalding water that will sever their intestines?
>
> (Qur'ān, Muḥammad, 47:15)

Some might be wondering, why a river of wine is in *Jannah* when Allah (s.w.t.) has forbidden us to consume alcohol. Yes, indeed it is true that Allah has prohibited us from consuming alcohol and wine in this *dunya*, but the *khamr* in *Jannah* is different. The *khamr*, the wine in *Jannah* does not give us a headache nor does it make us intoxicated. This is mentioned in the following verse in the Qur'ān:

لَّا يُصَدَّعُونَ عَنْهَا وَلَا يُنزِفُونَ ﴿١٩﴾

> No headache will they have therefrom, nor will they be intoxicated—
>
> (Qur'ān, al-Waqi'ah, 56:19)

SubḥānAllāh.

Additionally, these four rivers spring forth from

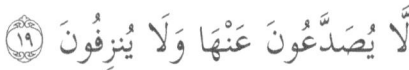

Jannatul-Firdaws, beneath the *'Arsh* of Allah the Almighty:

'Ubadah bin aṣ-Ṣamit narrated that the Messenger of Allah (s.a.w) said:

"In Paradise, there are a hundred levels, what is between every two levels is like what is between the heavens and the earth. *Al-Firdaws* is its highest level, and from it, the four rivers of Paradise are made to flow forth. So when you ask Allah, ask Him for *al-Firdaws*."

(Jami' at-Tirmidhi 2531)

One of the rivers of *Jannah* is also described in a sound hadith—the river of *al-Kawthar*, the river that has been granted to the Prophet Muḥammad (s.a.w.). It is described that the river's banks are made of gold and its soil is more fragrant than the musk while the water is sweeter than honey and whiter than snow:

It was narrated from Ibn 'Umar that the Messenger of Allah (s.a.w) said:

"*Kawthar* is a river in Paradise whose banks are of gold and its bed is of rubies and pearls. Its soil is more fragrant than musk, its water is sweeter than honey and whiter than snow."

(Sunan ibn Majah 4334)

Kawthar is a river in Paradise whose banks are of gold and its bed is of rubies and pearls.

Its soil is more fragrant than musk, its water is sweeter than honey and whiter than snow.

CHAPTER 7

The Fragrance of *Jannah*

Let us now delve into—عرف الجنة—*ʿarf al-Jannah.*

It is mentioned in the hadith that the fragrance of heaven—*ʿarf al-Jannah*—can be smelt at the distance of travelling for 500 years.

It was narrated from ʿAbdullah bin ʿAmr that the Messenger of Allah (s.a.w.) said:

> "Whoever claims to belong to someone other than his father will not smell the fragrance of Paradise, even though its fragrance may be detected from a distance of five hundred years."
>
> (Sunan ibn Majah 2611)

Additionally, there will also be some people who will not be able to smell the scent of *Jannah*. These are the people who falsely ascribe a lineage to themselves, kill the *Ahl Adh-Dhimmah*, kill the *mu'ahid* who has the protection of Allah and His Messenger (s.a.w.), seek knowledge not for the pleasure of Allah but for the benefit of the *dunya*, women who reveal their body and wear tight clothes and more. These are mentioned in the hadiths below:

Abu Hurayrah (r.a.) said:

> The Messenger of Allah (s.a.w.) said, "A person who acquires (religious) knowledge, which is (normally) acquired to gain the Pleasure of Allah, (for the sole reason) to secure worldly comforts will not even smell the fragrance of *Jannah* on the Day of Resurrection (i.e., will not enter *Jannah*)."

(Riyaḍ aṣ-Ṣaliḥin 1620)

He reported God's Messenger as saying, "There are two classes of those who will go to Hell whom I have not seen":

> People with whips like ox-tails with which they strike people; and women with such clothing

> as to be virtually naked, who incite men and are inclined towards men, whose heads are like the swaying humps of Bactrian camels. Such women will not enter paradise or experience its fragrance, though its fragrance can be experienced at such and such a distance."
>
> (Mishkat al-Maṣabiḥ 3524)

And so, the euphoric fragrance of *Jannah* can be smelt from afar. That is why after the believers have been reckoned—when it is decided who will enter *Jannah*—those believers will smell the scent of *Jannah* way before they even come close to *Jannah*, even way before the gates of *Jannah*.

The fragrance of *Jannah* will be smelt by the dwellers of *Jannah* from a distance of 500 years

CHAPTER 8

The Gates of *Jannah*

Dear brothers and sisters, which gate would you like to enter *Jannah* with?

Do you know how many gates there are for *Jannah*? There are eight gates of *Jannah*.

The Prophet (s.a.w.) mentioned that there are eight gates of *Jannah* and seven gates of *an-Naar*. Furthermore, it is also mentioned in the hadith below that there will be a gate called *ar-Rayyan*, and it is for those who excel in fasting.

Narrated Sahl bin Sa'd:

> The Prophet (s.a.w.) said, "Paradise has eight gates, and one of them is called *Ar-Rayyan* through which none will enter but those who observe fasting."
>
> (Ṣaḥiḥ al-Bukhari 3257)

These people did not only fast in the beautiful sacred month of Ramadan but also on Mondays and Thursdays, al-*Ayyam al-Biḍ*—every 13,14 and 15 of the lunar months, the day of 'Arafah, the day of 'Ashura' and more. Because these believers were righteous in their fasting, there will be a gate exclusively for them, and they will be called upon to enter the eternal abode of bliss through this gate.

But that is just one gate. What about the others? The other gates of *Jannah* are *Baab aṣ-Ṣadaqah*, for those who excelled in giving charity and *Baab al-Jihad* for the *mujahidin*. There are gates for each of the righteous deeds, and the believers will be called upon from the gate by the deed they triumphed in.

In essence, whoever excels in a particular deed, will be invited to enter *Jannah* from that gate of the deed they excelled in.

Dear readers, do you think there will be believers who will be called upon from all the gates of *Jannah*? The answer is yes, and one of them is Sayyidina Abu Bakr (r.a.). When the Prophet (s.a.w.) mentioned the eight gates of *Jannah*, Sayyidina Abu Bakr (r.a.) asked a question that many would not have asked. He (r.a.) asked, "Ya Rasulullah (s.a.w.), will there be a person who will be called upon to enter *Jannah* from all the gates?" The Prophet (s.a.w.) gave him a beautiful answer and said, "Yes indeed. And I hope you, Abu Bakr, will be the one."

Narrated Abu Hurayrah:

> I heard Allah's Messenger (s.a.w.) saying, "Anybody who spends a pair of something in Allah's cause will be called from all the gates of Paradise, 'O' Allah's slave! This is good.' He who is amongst those who pray will be called from the gate of the prayer (in Paradise) and he who is from the people of *Jihad* will be called from the gate of *Jihad*, and he who is from those who give in charity (i.e. *Zakah*) will be called from the gate of charity, and he who is amongst those who observe fast will be called from the gate of fasting, the gate

> of *Rayyan*." Abu Bakr said, "He who is called from all those gates will need nothing," He added, "Will anyone be called from all those gates, O' Allah's Messenger (s.a.w.)?" He said, "Yes, and I hope you will be among those, O' Abu Bakr."
>
> (Ṣaḥiḥ al-Bukhari 3666)

Why did the Prophet (s.a.w.) say that to Abu Bakr (r.a.)? Because Abu Bakr (r.a.) was someone who excelled in every field by the grace of Allah. This shows us an insight into the *ṣaḥabah* of the Prophet (s.a.w.), whereby the companions aimed very high and inspired and strived to be the best. They did not just settle and sit in for anything or the minimum. They aimed very high, unlike us who just pray to simply enter *Jannah*.

However, the Prophet (s.a.w.) himself taught them and us not to settle for less and to aim high. He (s.a.w.) said that whenever we ask Allah for Paradise, do not settle for the minimum. Instead, aim high—ask and pray to Allah for *Jannatul-Firdaws*. So, ask for *Jannatul-Firdaws*, dear readers.

Furthermore, the Prophet (s.a.w.) mentioned in a hadith that *mashā'Allāh,* the distance between the two sides of each gate—the width of each gate—is a travel distance of forty years, yet it will be very crowded when the believers are entering the gates.

> ...We have been informed (i.e., by the Prophet (s.a.w) that the distance between two shutters of the gate of *Jannah* is forty years (distance). And a day would come when it would be fully packed...
>
> (Riyaḍ aṣ-Ṣaliḥin 497)

Which gate would you like to enter *Jannah* with?

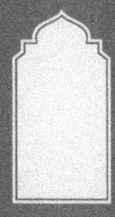

Baab as-Ṣalah Those who are punctual and focused in their prayers	***Baab al-Jihad*** Those who have died in the defence of Islam
Baab as-Ṣadaqah Those who frequently give to charity	***Baab ar-Rayyan*** Those who constantly fast to obtain the blessings of Allah

Baab al-Ḥajj

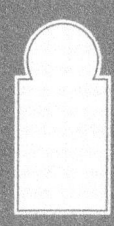

Those who observe the pilgrimage

Baab al-Kaẓimin al-Ghaiẓ wal-'Afina 'anin-Naas

Those who suppress their anger and forgive others

Baab al-Iman

Those who have sincere faith and trust in Allah

Baab al-Dhikr

Those who constantly and excessively keep their tongues moist with the remembrance of Allah

CHAPTER 9

The Levels in *Jannah*

I mentioned in the previous chapter that the Prophet Muḥammad (s.a.w.) taught us that when we ask for *Jannah*, we should not settle for the minimum. Instead, we should aim high and ask for the highest level of *Jannah*—*Jannatul-Firdaws*. Why? Because there are a hundred levels in *Jannah*, and at the highest is *Jannatul-Firdaws*, which is below the *ʿArsh* of Allah the Almighty:

Muʿadh bin Jabal said:

> "I heard the Messenger of Allah (s.a.w.) say: 'Paradise has one hundred grades, each of which is as big as the distance between heaven and earth. The highest of them is *Firdaws*, and the best of them is *Firdaws*. The Throne

> is above *Firdaws* and from it springs forth the rivers of Paradise. If you ask of Allah, ask Him for *Firdaws*.'"
>
> (Sunan ibn Majah 4331)

Furthermore, in the above hadith, it is mentioned that the distance between each of the levels of *Jannah* is as wide as the distance between the heavens and the earth. Additionally, in another hadith, the distance between the two levels is said to be a distance of a hundred years as well.

Abu Hurayrah narrated that the Messenger of Allah (s.a.w) said:

> "In Paradise, there are a hundred levels, between every two levels is (the distance of) a hundred years."
>
> (Jami' at-Tirmidhi 2529)

Loved Ones in a Different Level in *Jannah*

I really love my wife and children so much, and I hope we will all be in *Jannah* together, *Inshā'Allāh*. And so, the reason why I send and put my children in programs where they can memorise the Qur'an and learn about the *deen* is so that we will all be in heaven. However, it is quite possible that we will not be on the same level in terms of our *iman*—which means that when we *inshā'Allāh* enter *Jannah*, we probably will not be on the same level.

And so, Allah (s.w.t.) mentions this beautiful verse in the Qur'an:

وَٱلَّذِينَ ءَامَنُوا۟ وَٱتَّبَعَتْهُمْ ذُرِّيَّتُهُم بِإِيمَـٰنٍ
أَلْحَقْنَا بِهِمْ ذُرِّيَّتَهُمْ وَمَآ أَلَتْنَـٰهُم مِّنْ
عَمَلِهِم مِّن شَىْءٍ ۚ كُلُّ ٱمْرِئٍۭ بِمَا
كَسَبَ رَهِينٌ ﴿٢١﴾

And those who believed and whose descendants followed them in faith—We will join with them their descendants, and We will

> not deprive them of anything of their deeds. Every person, for what he earned, is retained.
>
> (Qur'an, aṭ-Ṭur, 52:21)

SubḥānAllāh. This verse from surah aṭ-Ṭur is very lovely.

'Abdullah ibn Abbas once mentioned in a hadith about the verse above. He (r.a.) mentioned that when the believer and his family enter *Jannah*, they might be on different levels. The believer is perhaps on the higher level, and his family is on the lower level. And so, to please the believer's heart, Allah the Almighty will make the believer's entire family, descendants, offspring, and his or her spouse be upgraded to the higher level of *Jannah* so that they can join him/her. *SubḥānAllāh.* It is not the other way around—whereby the one who is at the higher level will go to the lower level. No. Allah will make those who are in the lower level be upgraded to the higher level so that they can be together with their loved ones:

> Ath-Thawri reported that Ibn 'Abbas said, "Verily, Allah elevates the ranks of the believers' offspring to the rank of their parents, even though the latter has not performed

> as well as the former so that the eyes of the parents are comforted." Ibn 'Abbas then recited this *ayah*: And those who believe and whose offspring follow them in Faith, to them shall We join their offspring, and We shall not decrease the reward of their deeds in anything (at-Tur 52:21).
>
> (Tafsir ibn Kathir 7/402)

In essence, there will be believers who will not be on the same level as their families and loved ones in *Jannah*. This is because even though their family is righteous, it is quite possible that they are not on the same level in terms of their *iman*. Some might have loved ones and families who are not as righteous as they are. And so, their families will be placed in a lower level in *Jannah*. However, to please the believers' hearts who are at the higher level in *Jannah*, Allah will upgrade their families to their level so that they can be together.

Allah will comfort the eyes of the parents by seeing their offspring elevated to their grades.

Surely, Allah will gather them together in the best manner.

He will not decrease the reward or the grades of those higher in rank for joining them together.

CHAPTER 10

The Last People to Enter *Jannah*

It was narrated from Sahl bin Saʿd that the Messenger of Allah (s.a.w.) said:

> "A place the size of a whip in Paradise is better than this world and everything in it."
>
> (Sunan ibn Majah 4330)

What does this hadith mean? It means that a place that is small in *Jannah* like the size of a whip, is better than anything in this whole wide world and what it contains.

So, this will now take us to learn about the share of the person who will receive the least and the share of the person who will receive the most in *Jannah*.

Thus, let us now dive into the last people who will

enter *Jannah*—the people of *Jahannam*. The Prophet (s.a.w.) mentioned in a hadith, "I have been made aware of the last people who will enter Paradise."

Who is it, dear brothers and sisters?

Who are the last people to enter Jannah?

It is the people whose bad deeds outweigh their good deeds.

These people will first enter *an-Naar*—Hellfire to be purified from their sins. After their sins have been cleansed, Allah will pardon and forgive them. They will then be taken out of *Jahannam* by Allah's mercy and will be sent to *Jannah*.

Allah will say to the servant, "*'Abdi* enter My *Jannah* now by My mercy." The servant will come to the door of *Jannah* whilst thinking that it is full. The servant will then say, "O'Allah, there is no room for me. It is full."

On a side note, I mentioned that these are the people who will enter *Jannah* last, meaning it is not just one person. Furthermore, as a matter of fact, the Prophet (s.a.w.) called these people *al-Jahannamiyyin* because they spent some time in *Jahannam*. They are the people who were first burnt in *Jahannam*, and then Allah saved them as He (s.w.t.) had mercy on them.

It was narrated from ʿAbdullah bin Masʿud that the Messenger of Allah (s.a.w.) said:

> "I know the last of the people of Hell who will be brought forth from it, and the last of the people of Paradise to be admitted to Paradise. (It is) a man who will emerge from Hell crawling, and it will be said to him: 'Go and enter Paradise.' He will come to it and it will be made to appear to him as if it is full. Allah will say: 'Go and enter Paradise.' He will come to it and it will appear to him as if it is full. So he will say: 'O' Lord, I found it full.' Allah will say: 'Go and enter Paradise.' He will come to it and it will be made to appear to him as if it is full. So he will say: 'O' Lord, I found it full.' Allah will say: 'Go and enter Paradise, for you will have the like of the world and ten times more, or you will have ten times the like of the world.' He will say: 'Are You mocking me, or are You laughing at me, when You are the Sovereign?'" He said: "And I saw the Messenger of Allah (s.a.w.) smiling

so broadly that his molar teeth could be seen." And he used to say: "This is the lowest of the people of Paradise in status."

(Sunan ibn Majah 4339)

Back to the hadith, Allah will tell the servant, "Enter *Jannah*. You have a share in it." Allah will also then ask, "How much would you like to have in *Jannah*? Would you like Me to give you as much as the entire world and what it contains?"

Many of us today dream of having the biggest house in a beautiful neighbourhood, a luxurious car, a beautiful family, a decent bank account and more. However, all these things are nothing compared to what we can get in *Jannah*. This whole *dunya* and what it contains, is just a small place in heaven—like the size of a whip. And so, when Allah is asking the *'Abdi* about how much he would like, the servant will say, "O'Allah are you mocking me? Are you making fun of me? You are the Lord of all creations."

Allah will then tell His servant, "I will give you similar to what the entire world contains but ten times more." *SubḥānAllāh,* ten times more than the likes of this *dunya* and what it contains will be given to him, and this is just the share of the dwellers of *Jannah* who will receive the least. Can you imagine the one who will receive the most—the ones who straight away enter *Jannah* first?

While citing this hadith, the Prophet (s.a.w.) was laughing until his molar teeth were visible. He (s.a.w.) laughed because the servant was arguing with Allah and Allah the Almighty allowed His servant to argue with Him. The Prophet (s.a.w.) also smiled because after Allah (s.w.t.) saves the servant from Hellfire, He will give them ten times more of this *dunya* and what it contains.

In essence, the people who have committed a lot of sins and have their bad deeds outweigh their good deeds will be first sent to *Jahannam*. And then by Allah's mercy, they will be saved from the blazing fire. Afterwards, Allah will shower them with the blessing of receiving ten times more of this *dunya* and what it contains which is the least share for the dwellers of heaven. So, what do you think will be the share of the righteous people who will make it to heaven first? What more for them?

A small place
equal to an area
occupied by a whip
in *Jannah* is better
than the whole
world and whatever
is in it

CHAPTER 11

The Two *Bisharah*

Dear brothers and sisters, I would like to share with you two *bisharah*—two pieces of good news pertaining to *Jannah*.

In the hadiths, the Prophet (s.a.w.) mentioned two *bisharah*, and these two *bisharah* are in different hadiths. The hadiths have their similarities, but the *bisharah* are different.

Let us delve into the first *bisharah* that is narrated by Abu Saʿid al-Khudri. The Prophet (s.a.w.) mentioned in a hadith that when the *ahlul-Jannah* make it to heaven and settle themselves there, Allah will ask them, "Ya *Ahlul-Jannah*, O' People of Heaven, are you happy? Do you wish for anything more?" The dwellers of *Jannah* will say, "O' Allah, what could be more than all this that You have given? Have You not brightened our faces? Have You not forgiven our sins?

Have you not admitted us to your *Jannah*? Have you not saved us from Hellfire? What more is there?"

Allah will tell them, "Yes, there is more." Allah will then say, "I will be pleased with you. I will never be displeased with you at all." *SubḥānAllāh.*

On the authority of Abu Saʿid al-Khudri (r.a.), who said that the Messenger of Allah (s.a.w.) said:

> Allah will say to the inhabitants of Paradise: O' inhabitants of Paradise! They will say: O' our Lord, we present ourselves and are at Your pleasure, and goodness rests in Your hands. Then He will say: Are you content? And they will say: And how should we not be content, O' Lord when You have given to us that which You have given to no one else of Your creation? Then He will say: Would you not like Me to give you something better than that? And they will say: O' Lord and what thing is better than that? And He will say: I shall cause My favour to descend upon you and thereafter shall never be displeased with you.

(Hadith 40, 40 Hadith Qudsi)

The second *bisharah* is by Imam Muslim. The hadith is similar, but the part after Allah says, "There is more," is different. In the hadith by Imam Muslim, after Allah says, "There is more," Allah the Almighty removes the veil.

Allah will remove the veil, and the dwellers of *Jannah* will lay their eyes on Allah. These dwellers of *Jannah* will get to see the Almighty Allah and *subḥānAllāh*, dear brothers and sisters—this is the greatest reward ever for the believers.

Ṣuhaib reported the Apostle (s.a.w.) saying:

> When those deserving of Paradise would enter Paradise, the Blessed and the Exalted would ask: "Do you wish Me to give you anything more?" They would say: "Hast Thou not brightened our faces? Hast Thou not made us enter Paradise and saved us from Fire?" He (the narrator) said: "He (God) would lift the veil, and of things given to them nothing would be dearer to them than the sight of their Lord, the Mighty and the Glorious."

(Ṣaḥiḥ Muslim 181a)

Whoever loves to
meet Allah,
Allah loves to
meet him,
and whoever
hates to meet Allah,
Allah hates to
meet him

CHAPTER 12

The Light of *Jannah*

وُجُوهٌ يَوْمَئِذٍ نَّاضِرَةٌ ﴿٢٢﴾ إِلَىٰ رَبِّهَا نَاظِرَةٌ ﴿٢٣﴾

[Some] faces, that Day, will be radiant, Looking at their Lord.

(Qur'an, al-Qiyamah, 75:22-23)

On the Day of Judgement, some faces will be so bright and radiant—their faces will be covered with the light of Allah as they look upon Him (s.w.t.).

The faces of the believers will be radiant, and they will be glowing like the full moon as they are filled with joy and happiness because they are meeting with Allah the Almighty. It is mentioned in a hadith that the Prophet (s.a.w.) said that some of the faces of the people will be bright like the moon on a full night:

Abu Hurayrah reported:

> The Messenger of Allah (s.a.w.) said: "Seventy thousand (persons) would enter Paradise as one group and among them (there would be people) whose faces would be bright like the moon."
>
> (Ṣaḥiḥ Muslim 217)

In another hadith, the Prophet (s.a.w.) mentioned that the people who first enter *Jannah* will also be glittering like the full moon:

Narrated Abu Hurayrah:

> Allah's Messenger (s.a.w) said, "The first group of people who will enter Paradise will be glittering like the full moon and those who will follow them will glitter like the most brilliant star in the sky. They will not urinate, relieve nature, spit, or have any nasal secretions. Their combs will be of gold, and their sweat will smell like musk. The aloes-wood will be used in their centres. Their wives will be houris. All of them will look alike and

> will resemble their father Adam (in stature), sixty cubits tall."
>
> (Ṣaḥiḥ al-Bukhari 3327)

Why will the believers' faces radiate like the full moon? Because they get to see Allah the Almighty.

It was narrated that Jabir bin 'Abdullah said:

> "The Messenger of Allah said: 'While the people of Paradise are enjoying their blessings, a light will shine upon them, and they will raise their heads, and they will see their Lord looking upon them from above. He will say: "Peace be upon you, O' people of Paradise." This is what Allah says in the verse: "*Salam* (peace be upon you)—a Word from the Lord (Allah), The Most Merciful." He will look at them, and they will look at Him, and they will not pay any attention to the delights (of Paradise) so long as they look at Him until He will screen Himself from them. But His light and blessing will remain with them in their bodies.'"
>
> (Sunan ibn Majah 184)

Will we all have the same access to this in *Jannah*? Will we all have the same access to the *bisharah* that I mentioned in the previous chapter? No. In *Jannah*, the believers will have different access to meeting Allah.

Some of the believers will get to see Allah (s.w.t.) on a daily basis, and some will get to see Him on a weekly basis. Some will get to see Him once a year, and so on based on their level of good deeds and bad deeds.

In essence, Allah is the light of *Jannah*.

Allah is the Light of the heavens and the earth.

His light is like a niche in which there is a lamp,

the lamp is in a crystal,

the crystal is like a shining star,

lit from the oil of a blessed olive tree,

located neither to the east nor the west,

whose oil would almost glow,

even without being touched by fire

CHAPTER 13

The Delights of *Jannah*

Dear brothers and sisters, I would like to share some more good news.

Mashā'Allāh, everything about *Jannah* is filled with beauty and great news. The Almighty Allah mentions in the Qur'an that once we enter heaven, once we set foot in heaven, we will be free from any fatigue:

لَا يَمَسُّهُمْ فِيهَا نَصَبٌ وَمَا هُم مِّنْهَا بِمُخْرَجِينَ ﴿٤٨﴾

No fatigue will touch them therein, nor from it will they [ever] be removed.

(Qur'an, al-Ḥijr, 15:48)

Additionally, in the same verse, Allah also mentions another piece of great news, which is that whatever we wish for will not be removed when we are in the eternal abode of bliss.

What does this mean? Let me give an example. In this *dunya*, once we, for instance, achieve our goals of getting our dream car, dream house, or dream job—we tend to be happy and worried. Why? Why are we worried? Shouldn't we just be happy since we have already achieved what we wanted? Why? Because we are afraid that we will lose it.

We are afraid that one day, it will be removed from our lives. We are afraid that our dream will shatter once we are unable to come up with the mortgage for the house. Or we lose our loved ones, which will then consequently ruin the happiness, joy and pleasures of life.

There is always the fear and worry factors present in ourselves. We are constantly worried that something might happen. We are worried that we will lose all the things that we have achieved, or we are worried that we will depart from this life and leave all the luxuries and extravagance behind.

However, the thing is, dear brothers and sisters,

when we enter *Jannah*, once we set foot in *Jannah*—this worry would disappear, this worry would not be there at all. This is because we would not lose anything when we are in eternal bliss. Once the *ahlul-Jannah* enters Paradise and the *ahlun-Naar* enters Hellfire, Allah will create death in the form of a ram. And He (s.w.t.) will slaughter it between *al-Jannah* and *an-Naar*. Afterwards, He (s.w.t.) will declare to *ahlul-Jannah*, "You will live eternally in heaven. You have an eternal abode in heaven, and there is no death no more." The similar thing will also be said to the dwellers of Hellfire:

Narrated Abu Sa'id Al-Khudri:

Allah's Messenger (s.a.w.) said, "On the Day of Resurrection, Death will be brought forward in the shape of a black and white ram. Then a call maker will call, 'O' people of Paradise!' Thereupon they will stretch their necks and look carefully. The caller will say, 'Do you know this?' They will say, 'Yes, this is Death.' By then all of them will have seen it. Then it will be announced again, 'O' people of Hell!' They will stretch their necks and look carefully. The caller will say, 'Do you know this?' They will say, 'Yes, this is Death.' And by then all of them will have seen it. Then it (that ram) will be slaughtered and the caller will say, 'O' people of Paradise! Eternity for you and no death O' people of Hell! Eternity for you and no death.'" Then the Prophet (s.a.w.) recited: "And warn them of the Day of distress when the case has been decided, while (now) they are in a state of carelessness (i.e. the people of the world) and they do not believe." (19.39)

(Ṣaḥiḥ al-Bukhari 4730)

May Allah protect us against the Hellfire. May Allah grant us His mercy to enter His *Jannah*.

In essence, one of the greatest joys and delights of *Jannah* is that we are assured that there will be no fatigue and everything is forever:

خَٰلِدِينَ فِيهَآ أَبَدًاۚ إِنَّ ٱللَّهَ عِندَهُۥٓ أَجۡرٌ عَظِيمٞ ﴿٢٢﴾

[They will be] abiding therein forever. Indeed, Allah has with Him a great reward.

(Qur'an, at-Tawbah, 9:22)

The life of this world
is no more than
the delusion of
enjoyment.
Death is certain
and life is not.
But *Jannah* is
eternal.

CHAPTER 14

The Comfort of *Jannah*

In relation to the previous chapter, the joy of *Jannah* is that we are assured that everything is forever:

خَٰلِدِينَ فِيهَآ أَبَدًا ۚ إِنَّ ٱللَّهَ عِندَهُۥٓ أَجْرٌ عَظِيمٌ ﴿٢٢﴾

[They will be] abiding therein forever. Indeed, Allah has with Him a great reward.

(Qur'an, at-Tawbah, 9:22)

This is the comfort of *Jannah* as well. That is why when Imam Aḥmad was asked, "When do we experience comfort?" He (r.a.) said, "Once we set our foot in *Jannah*. Not before that":

> Imam Aḥmad bin Ḥanbal was asked: "When does a servant truly taste the joy of rest?" He replied: "When the first foot enters *Jannah* (Paradise)"
>
> (Ṭabaqat al-Ḥanabilah 1/293)

The *dunya*, the place before *Jannah*, is filled with trials and tests. That is what life is all about.

In a sound hadith, the Prophet (s.a.w.) mentioned that on the Day of Judgement, when the people who suffered immensely in this *dunya* are dipped into *Jannah* for a short moment, they will say, "O' Allah, I did not suffer even one bit in *dunya*:"

Anas bin Malik reported that Allah's Messenger (s.a.w.) said that one amongst the denizens of Hell who had led a life of ease and plenty amongst the people of the world would be made to dip in Fire only once on the Day of Resurrection and then it would be said to him:

> "O' son of Adam, did you find any comfort, did you happen to get any material blessing?" He would say: "By Allah, no, my Lord." And then that person from amongst the persons of the world be brought who had led the most

> miserable life (in the world) from amongst the inmates of Paradise. And he would be made to dip once in Paradise, and it would be said to him, "O' son of Adam, did you face any hardship? Or had any distress fallen to your lot?" And he would say: "By Allah, no, my Lord, never did I face any hardship or experience any distress."
>
> (Ṣaḥiḥ Muslim 2807)

For me, those who are suffering the most right now are our brothers and sisters in Palestine. May Allah bless them. May Allah grant them victory. May Allah defeat their enemies and humiliate them. May Allah save and spare our brothers and sisters in Palestine, *āmīn*. They are the true *mujahidin*. They are defenders and the honour of the entire *ummah*. They have been suffering the most at the hands of the enemies of Allah and His prophets.

On the Day of Judgement, the person who suffered the most in this *dunya* will be resurrected by Allah. The righteous and true believers will be eligible to enter heaven. However, before that, they will have a quick tour of heaven on the Day of Resurrection. As mentioned in the hadith, Allah will tell his angels

"*Al-ghams*"—meaning to immerse. He (s.w.t.) will order the angels to immerse, to dip the believers into heaven momentarily. Why? To give them a quick tour and feel of *Jannah*. After they have been immersed in *Jannah*, they will be taken out. Allah will then ask them, "Ya *'abdi*, My servant, did you ever suffer any hardship or difficulty? Have you ever experienced any test or trial?" The *'abdi* will say, "I swear to you, Allah, I have been enjoying my life ever since I was born."

The believers who suffered immensely will say that. Why? Because when they are dipped into heaven for that brief moment, they will see what Allah has prepared for them—and they are certain that it would be their dwelling place forever. That quick tour in *Jannah*, that brief moment of comfort, makes them forget all the hardships they experienced—all the trials, disease, sickness, poverty, and persecution they experienced are forgotten. That is why they will say, "I swear to you, Allah, I have been enjoying my life ever since I was born. I have not seen any hardship nor distress."

That is why when the rock was put on Bilal's (r.a.) chest and the disbelievers wanted him to say the word of disbelief, he did not do so. He persevered and said,

"*Aḥadun aḥad,*" which means, "One, the only One." The disbelievers thought they could make him and force him to say the words of disbelief by implementing all the excruciating pain through that rock but he did not budge. He knew that the reward that awaited him was far more valuable than the trials of life.

In the same hadith, Allah (s.w.t) also mentions the people who lived lavishly in this *dunya*. On the Day of Judgement, Allah will bring forth the people who lived in luxury—the ones on the Forbes list, billionaires, the untouchable people. These people had everything they ever wanted and more, but they did not believe in Allah. They never thanked Allah, nor praised the Almighty Allah, and so they will be among the *ahlun-Naar* on the Day of Judgement.

Allah will order the angels to immerse them into Hellfire for a moment and then take them out. Afterwards, Allah will ask them, "Ya *'abdi*, My servant, did you ever enjoy anything in your life?" The servants will say, "I swear to you O' Allah, that I have been suffering ever since I was born."

All the years that were spent lavishly for sixty, eighty years will be forgotten by those people. Why? Because they were dipped into Hellfire for a brief moment, and they realised that it is a place where there is no salvation. That is why Allah says in surah Ali-ʿImran:

كُلُّ نَفْسٍ ذَآئِقَةُ ٱلْمَوْتِ ۗ وَإِنَّمَا تُوَفَّوْنَ أُجُورَكُمْ يَوْمَ ٱلْقِيَٰمَةِ ۖ فَمَن زُحْزِحَ عَنِ ٱلنَّارِ وَأُدْخِلَ ٱلْجَنَّةَ فَقَدْ فَازَ ۗ وَمَا ٱلْحَيَوٰةُ ٱلدُّنْيَآ إِلَّا مَتَٰعُ ٱلْغُرُورِ ﴿١٨٥﴾

Every soul will taste death, and you will only be given your [full] compensation on the Day of Resurrection. So he who is drawn away from the Fire and admitted to Paradise has attained [his desire]. And what is the life of this world except the enjoyment of delusion.

(Qur'an, Ali-ʿImran, 3:185)

Is there going to be someone who will not die? No. Every soul shall taste death. Every soul will receive their wages in full on the Day of Judgement.

Allah (s.w.t.) also mentions in the verse above that the person who is pushed away from Hellfire and enters Paradise safely is the one who has achieved the ultimate success.

What about the success of this life and what it contains? The success of *dunya* is temporary. It is the joy of deception and illusion because we cannot maintain it and possess it forever. It is short and brief. Eternal happiness is once we set our foot in *Jannah, inshā'Allāh.*

In *Jannah*, there is no fatigue, no stress, no pain, no hatred, and no negative feelings.

In *Jannah*, there is only peace.

In *Jannah*, there is everlasting happiness.

PART 3

The Footsteps of the True Believers

CHAPTER 15

The One Who Grieved When Separated

In the earlier chapters, I had touched upon the levels in *Jannah*, whereby we might not be on the same level in *Jannah* with our loved ones. This concern was also shared by one of the companions, Thawban ibn Bujdud (r.a.), who was one of the servants of the Prophet Muḥammad (s.a.w.).

'A'isyah (r.a.) narrated that once Thawban (r.a.) came to the Prophet (s.a.w.) whilst feeling down. The Prophet (s.a.w.) noticed his pale, fatigued look, and asked him why he was down. Thawban (r.a.) said, "Ya Rasulullah, I am not ill nor in pain. I was restless as I was unable to see you. Ya Rasulullah, by Allah, you are dearest to me than my own self. I love you more than I love myself. I love you more than my wealth. I love you more than my wife and children. I miss you when I am not with you. I grieve when I am not near you."

Basically, what Thawban (r.a.) was saying is that he missed the Prophet (s.a.w.) when he (s.a.w.) was not around him. At times, Thawban (r.a.) was away from the Prophet (s.a.w.) to fulfil his duties, and during that time, he missed the presence of the Prophet (s.a.w.). Even during the intervals of the five daily prayers, he (r.a.) missed him (s.a.w.). That is why during the five daily prayers in the masjid, Thawban (r.a.) was excited and filled with joy as he got to be near the Prophet (s.a.w.)—he got to lay his eyes on him (s.a.w.).

Thawban (r.a.) then said to the Prophet (s.a.w.), "Every time I remember that you will die, and I too will die, I fear that I will not be able to see you in the Hereafter. Even if I make it into heaven, I will not have access to see you as you will be placed at the highest level—*Jannatul-Firdaws*, and you will be placed among the other prophets. I won't have the same access to looking at you in *Jannah* as I can in this *dunya*."

When Thawban (r.a.) said that, the Prophet (s.a.w.) kept quiet as he (s.a.w.) could not promise him nor anyone that they will be with him (s.a.w.)

in *Jannatul-Firdaws*, because that is only up to Allah the Almighty. And so, at that moment, Allah (s.w.t.) revealed a beautiful verse:

وَمَن يُطِعِ ٱللَّهَ وَٱلرَّسُولَ فَأُوْلَٰٓئِكَ مَعَ
ٱلَّذِينَ أَنْعَمَ ٱللَّهُ عَلَيْهِم مِّنَ ٱلنَّبِيِّـۧنَ
وَٱلصِّدِّيقِينَ وَٱلشُّهَدَآءِ وَٱلصَّٰلِحِينَ ۚ
وَحَسُنَ أُوْلَٰٓئِكَ رَفِيقًا ٦٩

And whoever obeys Allah and the Messenger—those will be with the ones upon whom Allah has bestowed favour of the prophets, the steadfast affirmers of truth, the martyrs and the righteous. And excellent are those as companions.

(Qur'an, an-Nisa', 4:69)

In essence, whoever obeys Allah and the Messenger (s.a.w.) will be rewarded as follows: They will be gathered in *Jannah* with the company of the prophets, the *aṣ-ṣiddiqin* like Abu Bakr (r.a.), the *shuhada'* like Ḥamzah (r.a.), and all the righteous believers.

Mashā'Allāh. How excellent is such a company!

In *Jannah*, we
will be with those
whom we love.

CHAPTER 16

The One Who Truly Loved

Anas ibn Malik mentioned that there was once a time when he and the Prophet (s.a.w.) were leaving the *masjid*, and then a Bedouin came. He asked the Prophet (s.a.w.), "Ya Rasulullah (s.a.w.), when is the Day of Judgement?" The Prophet (s.a.w.) answered him with a question, "What have you prepared for it?" The man said, "Not much. I have not prepared many prayers, fasting, or charity. But I really and truly love Allah (s.w.t.) and His Messenger (s.a.w.)." To that, the Prophet (s.a.w.) replied, "You will be in the company of those whom you love on the Day of Judgement."

Narrated Anas (r.a.):

> A man asked the Prophet (s.a.w.) about the Hour (i.e. Day of Judgement), saying, "When will the Hour be?" The Prophet (s.a.w.) said, "What have you prepared for it?" The man said, "Nothing, except that I love Allah and His Apostle." The Prophet (s.a.w.) said, "You will be with those whom you love." We had never been so glad as we were on hearing that saying of the Prophet (i.e., "You will be with those whom you love.") Therefore, I love the Prophet, Abu Bakr and 'Umar, and I hope that I will be with them because of my love for them though my deeds are not similar to theirs.
>
> (Ṣaḥiḥ al-Bukhari 3688)

Dear brothers and sisters, genuinely loving Allah and the Prophet (s.a.w.) is different from just saying, "I love the Prophet (s.a.w.). I love Allah. I love the Qur'an. I love my *deen*."

Love will inspire us to follow in the footsteps of the Prophet's (s.a.w.) guidance as well as the sunnah. Truly loving him (s.a.w.) is when his (s.a.w.) name is mentioned, we say the peace and salutations upon him, we study the *sirah*, we practise his sunnah to the best of our ability and we do not ignore it.

Sometimes, people ask me, "Shaykh, is smoking haram or *makruh*?" When I ask them why, they will say, "Because if it is *makruh*, then it is okay for me to smoke." No. It is not okay. At times, people ask me questions about whether a certain act or deed is either sunnah or compulsory. And when I say that it is a sunnah they will say, "*Alḥamdulillāh.* Then I do not have to do it." 'A'isyah (r.a.) once mentioned that the Prophet (s.a.w.) used to interrupt and stop doing some good deeds consistently out of fear that his companions would perceive it as compulsory.

Narrated 'A'ishah, wife of Prophet (s.a.w.):

> The Messenger of Allah (s.a.w.) never offered prayer in the forenoon, but I offer it. The Messenger of Allah (s.a.w.) would give up an action, though he liked to do it, lest the people should continue it and it is prescribed for them.
>
> (Sunan Abi Dawud 1293)

What is it that we must understand from this hadith?

We must understand that the companions would copy the Prophet (s.a.w.) in everything that he (s.a.w.)

did. Even the sunnah acts done by the Prophet (s.a.w.) were seen and perceived as *fard* and something that must be done regularly.

That is why the Prophet (s.a.w.) did not pray the *ḍuḥa* regularly. Why? To make it clear to his (s.a.w.) *ummah* that it is not *wajib*—that it is a sunnah.

And so, look at how the companions perceived the sunnah as compared to us now. Nowadays, unfortunately, whenever we hear that it is a sunnah, we will say, "It is just a sunnah. I don't have to do it. It's okay if I ignore it." *Astagfirullāh.*

In essence, following the guidance of the Prophet Muḥammad (s.a.w.) is a sign of loving him (s.a.w.). And so that is why he (s.a.w.) said these words in the hadith narrated by Anas (r.a.):

أَنْتَ مَعَ مَنْ أَحْبَبْتَ

"You will be with those whom you love."

If we are true in what we say—about loving Allah and His Messenger (s.a.w.)—we will be gathered with the people whom we love on the Day of Judgement.

After hearing those words, the man said, "This is the greatest news that I have ever heard after accepting Islam." When asked why, he said, "I love Allah and His Messenger (s.a.w.). I love Abu Bakr (r.a.) and 'Umar (r.a.). And I hope to be gathered with them in heaven. Even though I'm not as good as them, I want to be with them as I love them."

Therefore, follow the footsteps of our beloved Messenger (s.a.w.) and his companions in doing the sunnah as well. We have to work hard for our *Jannah*. Faṭimah (r.a.) was also not exempted from this. She, too, was required to work hard for *Jannah*. The Prophet (s.a.w.) used to tell his daughter, Faṭimah (r.a.), "O' Faṭimah, you have to work hard to earn *Jannah*. You must do good deeds to be eligible to enter heaven. Just because you are my daughter, that does not mean that you will be granted *Jannah*. By Allah, I cannot avail you against Allah. You have to work hard."

Some people think that if they are a "*Syed*" or a descendant of the Prophet's (s.a.w.) lineage, they will be given a green pass to heaven. No, that is not right nor true. Even Faṭimah (r.a.), the beloved daughter of the Prophet (s.a.w.)—the one who is said to be the Chief of all women in Paradise was not exempted. The Prophet (s.a.w.) still told her to work hard and do good deeds to be eligible to enter *Jannah:*

Narrated Abu Hurayrah:

When Allah revealed the Verse: "Warn your nearest kinsmen," Allah's Messenger (s.a.w.) got up and said, "O' people of Quraysh (or said similar words)! Buy (i.e. save) yourselves (from the Hellfire) as I cannot save you from Allah's Punishment; O' Bani 'Abd Manaf! I cannot save you from Allah's Punishment; O' Ṣafiyyah, the Aunt of Allah's Messenger (s.a.w.)! I cannot save you from Allah's Punishment; O' Faṭimah bint Muḥammad! Ask me anything from my wealth, but I cannot save you from Allah's Punishment."

(Ṣaḥiḥ al-Bukhari 2753)

The Prophet Muḥammad (s.a.w.) once said:

Love Allah for what He nourishes you with of His Blessings,

love me due to the love of Allah,

and love the people of my house due to your love of me.

CHAPTER 17

The One Who Was Always in Prostration

Rabiʿah ibn Kaʿb al-Aslami (r.a.) was a companion who devoted himself to serving the Prophet (s.a.w.). Rabiʿah (r.a.) used to bring water to the Prophet (s.a.w.) so that he (s.a.w.) could make *wuḍu'* before the *Fajr* and *tahajjud* prayer. Due to his consistent actions and services, the Prophet (s.a.w.) wanted to reward him.

The Prophet (s.a.w.) said, "Rabiʿah, I want to reward you. Tell me. How should I reward you?" Rabiʿah (r.a.) told the Prophet (s.a.w.) that he would think about it first. After he thought about it, he went to the Prophet (s.a.w.) and said, "Ya Rasulullah (s.a.w.),

I want to be with you in *Jannah*, in the same place that you will be in." To this, the Prophet (s.a.w.) said, "I cannot afford to fulfil this request. Do you have any other requests?" Rabiʿah said, "No. That is it. That is what I would like." The Prophet (s.a.w.) then said, "Rabiʿah, help me achieve this status for you." Rabiʿah then asked, "How?" And the Prophet (s.a.w.) said, "*Kathratis-sujud*—by doing as much prostration as you could." Afterwards, Rabiʿah (r.a.) was always seen in prostration:

Rabiʿah ibn Kaʿb said:

> "I was with Allah's Messenger (s.a.w.) one night. And I brought him water and what he required. He said to me: 'Ask (anything you like).' I said: 'I ask your company in Paradise.' He (the Holy Prophet) said: 'Anything else besides it?' I said: 'That is all (what I require).' He said: 'Then help me to achieve this for you by devoting yourself often to prostration.'"
>
> (Ṣaḥiḥ Muslim 489)

What does this mean?

What does it mean to make plenty of *sujud*? It means to pray a lot.

It does not only mean the five daily prayers but also the sunnah prayers—such as the twelve sunnah prayers which I will be talking about in the next chapter.

The servant is closest to his *Rabb* during prostration.

So increase your supplications when prostrating.

PART 4

Acts and Supplications for *Jannah*

CHAPTER 18

Praying the 12 Sunnah Prayers

Umm Ḥabibah (r.a.), one of the Prophet's (s.a.w.) wife, one of the mothers of the believers, narrated the following hadith about the sunnah prayers:

Umm Ḥabibah narrated that Allah's Messenger (s.a.w.) said:

> "Whoever prays twelve *rak'ahs* in a day and night, a house will be built from him in Paradise: Four *rak'ahs* before *Ẓuhr*, two rak'ah after it, two *rak'ahs* after *Maghrib*, two *rak'ahs* after *'Isha'*, and two *rak'ahs* before *Fajr* in the morning *ṣalah*."

(Jamiʿ at-Tirmidhi 415)

As narrated in the hadith above, whoever observes praying the twelve sunnah prayers every day and night—Allah will build for him a house in the eternal abode of bliss.

In essence, dear brothers and sisters, follow in the footsteps of those before us—the Prophet (s.a.w.) and his companions—as the reward is beautiful. Having a house in *Jannah* is a beautiful offer by Allah the Almighty. So, take advantage of this wonderful offer.

As long as you are performing prayer, you are knocking at the door of Allah.

And whoever is knocking at the door of Allah, Allah will open it for him.

CHAPTER 19

Repeating after the *Mu'adhdhin*

Prophet Muḥammad (s.a.w.) mentioned in a hadith that when we hear the *Adhan*—the call to prayer, we should answer it—we should repeat after the *mu'adhdhin*.

Narrated Abu Sa'id Al-Khudri:

> Allah's Messenger (s.a.w.) said, "Whenever you hear the *Adhan*, say what the *mu'adh-dhin* is saying."

(Ṣaḥiḥ al-Bukhari 611)

Just for a moment, forget about phones, social media, TikTok, WhatsApp, Facebook, Instagram and so on. Instead, use that time for the sunnah prayer or for repeating after the *mu'adhdhin*. *SubḥānAllāh*, the reward for repeating after the *mu'adhdhin* is that *inshā'Allāh* we will be eligible to enter *Jannah*. If we sincerely repeat after the *mu'adhdhin*, we will be eligible to enter *Jannah*.

'Umar b. al-Khaṭṭab reported:

> The Messenger of Allah (s.a.w.) said: When the *mu'adhdhin*—the one making the call to prayer—says: Allah is the Greatest, Allah is the Greatest, and one of you should make this response: Allah is the Greatest, Allah is the Greatest; (and when the *mu'adhdhin*) says: I testify that there is no God but Allah, one should respond: I testify that there is no God but Allah, and when he says: I testify that Muḥammad is the Messenger of Allah, one should make a response: I testify that Muḥammad is Allah's Messenger. When he (the *mu'adhdhin*) says: Come to prayer, one should make a response: There is no might and no power except with Allah. When he (the *mu'adhdhin*) says: Come to salvation, one should respond: There is no might and no power except with Allah, and when he (the *mu'adhdhin*) says: Allah is the Greatest, Allah

> is the Greatest, then make a response: Allah is the Greatest, Allah is the Greatest. When he (the *mu'adhdhin*) says: There is no God but Allah, and he who makes a response from the heart: There is no God but Allah, he will enter Paradise.
>
> (Ṣaḥiḥ Muslim 385)

As I mentioned, having a house in *Jannah* is a beautiful offer by Allah the Almighty. Take advantage of this wonderful offer. Repeat after the *mu'adhdhin*. Even if we are reciting the Qur'an, fold our *muṣḥaf* and repeat after the *mu'adhdhin*. Do not recite the Qur'an while the *Adhan* is being called. Concentrate on the *Adhan* and repeat after the *mu'adhdhin*. When the *mu'adhdhin* says, "*Allāhu Akbar*," we too should say, "*Allāhu Akbar*."

Respond to the *Adhan*

Mu'adhdhin calls...	We respond...
اَللهُ أَكْبَرُ اَللهُ أَكْبَرُ Allah is the Greatest, Allah is the Greatest	اَللهُ أَكْبَرُ اَللهُ أَكْبَرُ Allah is the Greatest, Allah is the Greatest
أَشْهَدُ أَنْ لَّا إِلٰهَ إِلَّا اللهُ I bear witness that there is no God worthy to worship except Allah	أَشْهَدُ أَنْ لَّا إِلٰهَ إِلَّا اللهُ I bear witness that there is no God worthy to worship except Allah
أَشْهَدُ أَنَّ مُحَمَّدًا رَّسُولُ اللهِ I bear witness that Muḥammad is the Messenger of Allah	أَشْهَدُ أَنَّ مُحَمَّدًا رَّسُولُ اللهِ I bear witness that Muḥammad is the Messenger of Allah

حَيَّ عَلَى الصَّلَاةِ Come to *Ṣalaḥ*	لَا حَوْلَ وَلَا قُوَّةَ إِلَّا بِاللهِ There is no power or might except through Allah
حَيَّ عَلَى الْفَلَاحِ Come to success	لَا حَوْلَ وَلَا قُوَّةَ إِلَّا بِاللهِ There is no power or might except through Allah
اَللهُ أَكْبَرُ اَللهُ أَكْبَرُ Allah is the Greatest, Allah is the Greatest	اَللهُ أَكْبَرُ اَللهُ أَكْبَرُ Allah is the Greatest, Allah is the Greatest
لَا إِلٰهَ إِلَّا اللهُ There is no god worthy of worship except Allah	لَا إِلٰهَ إِلَّا اللهُ There is no god worthy of worship except Allah

No sound,

no call,

no voice is better

than the call of

Adhan.

CHAPTER 20

Du'a' after the *Adhan*

Narrated Jabir bin 'Abdullah:

> Allah's Messenger (s.a.w.) said, "Whoever, after listening to the *Adhan* (for the prayer), says, 'O' Allah, the Lord of this complete call and of this prayer, which is going to be established! Give Muḥammad *al-Wasilah* and *al-Faḍilah* and raise him to *al-Maqam al-Maḥmud*, which You have promised him,' will be granted my intercession for him on the Day of Resurrection."
>
> (Ṣaḥiḥ al-Bukhari 4719)

It is mentioned in the hadith that after the *Adhan* is finished, we should read the *du'a'* after the *Adhan*.

The following is the supplication that we must read after the *Adhan*:

اللَّهُمَّ رَبَّ هَذِهِ الدَّعْوَةِ التَّامَّةِ وَالصَّلَاةِ الْقَائِمَةِ آتِ مُحَمَّدًا الْوَسِيلَةَ وَالْفَضِيلَةَ وَابْعَثْهُ مَقَامًا مَحْمُودًا الَّذِي وَعَدْتَهُ

Allāhumma rabba hādhihid-daʿwatit-tāmmah, waṣ-ṣalātil-qāʾimah, ʾāti Muḥammadanil-wasīlata wal-faḍīlah, wabʿathhu maqāman maḥmūdanil-ladhī waʿadtah

O' Allah! Lord, of this perfect call (perfect by not ascribing partners to You) and of the regular prayer which is going to be established, give Muḥammad the right of intercession and illustriousness and resurrect him to the best and the highest place in Paradise that You promised him of.

(Ṣaḥiḥ al-Bukhari 614)

O' Allah, the Lord of this perfect supplication, the *Adhan*, the current prayer that we are going to offer, grant Muḥammad (s.a.w.) *al-Wasilah*.

What is *al-Wasilah?* It is the highest level in

Jannah, which is preserved for Prophet Muḥammad (s.a.w.). And so, when we make *du'a'* after the *Adhan, inshā'Allāh,* we will be granted his (s.a.w.) *shafa'ah*—intercession. The Prophet (s.a.w.) mentioned in the hadith above that, "Whoever supplicates after every *Adhan* will indeed be eligible for my intercession." So, memorise this *du'a'* by heart, dear brothers and sisters and recite it so that we will receive our beloved Prophet's (s.a.w.) intercession.

Connect to Allah's
line because
His line never
disconnects,
His line is never
busy,
His line doesn't
hang up.
Rather, His line is
always available.

CHAPTER 21

Du'a' after *Wuḍu'*

What is the *du'a'* that we should read after every *wuḍu'*? It is the following:

أَشْهَدُ أَنْ لاَ إِلَهَ إِلاَّ اللَّهُ وَحْدَهُ لاَ شَرِيكَ لَهُ وَأَشْهَدُ أَنَّ مُحَمَّدًا عَبْدُهُ وَرَسُولُهُ اللَّهُمَّ اجْعَلْنِي مِنَ التَّوَّابِينَ وَاجْعَلْنِي مِنَ الْمُتَطَهِّرِينَ

Ashhadu 'an lā ilāha 'illallāhu waḥdahu lā sharīka lah, wa 'ashhadu 'anna Muḥammadan 'abduhu wa rasūluh, Allāhumma-j'alnī minat-tawwābīn, wa-j'alnī minal-mutaṭahhirīn

> I testify that none has the right to be worshipped, but Allah alone, there are no partners for Him. And I testify that Muḥammad is His servant and Messenger. O' Allah! Make me among the repentants and make me among those who purify themselves.

Do you know what the beautiful reward is for reading this supplication? All the eight gates of *Jannah* will be opened for them, *subḥānAllāh*:

ʿUmar bin Al-Khaṭṭab narrated that:

> Allah's Messenger said: "Whoever performs *wuḍu'*, making *wuḍu'* well, then says: (*Ashhadu 'an lā ilāha 'illallāhu waḥdahu lā sharīka lah, wa 'ashhadu 'anna Muḥammadan ʿabduhu wa rasūluh, Allāhumma-jʿalnī minat-tawwābīn, wa-jʿalnī minal-mutaṭahhirīn*) 'I testify that none has the right to be worshipped but Allah alone, there are no partners for Him. And I testify that Muḥammad is His servant and Messenger. O' Allah! Make me among the repentants and make me among those who purify themselves.' Then eight gates of Paradise are opened for him, that may enter by whichever of them wishes."

(Jamiʿ at-Tirmidhi 55)

If we do not know the supplications, the *du'a's* by heart, then we must take action now. Know it, memorise it, comprehend it and recite it with all your heart. Ask Allah to make us among *at-Tawwabin*—those who frequently repent. Ask Allah to make us among *al-Mutaṭahhirin*—those who frequently purify themselves and repent.

Memorise and recite the above supplication after every *wuḍu'*, and *inshā'Allāh*, as mentioned in the hadith, the eight gates of *Jannah* will be opened widely, and the believers will be able to enter *Jannah* from whichever gate they wish. This is a very simple and easy thing to do, dear brothers and sisters.

Be busy working hard for our *Jannah*. Unfortunately, many of us are preoccupied with the *fitnah*—the test and trials—that we are living in today. We are all at the same dining table eating, but everyone is just looking at their phones. Is this not the reality? Sadly, it is. Whenever we are with our families and loved ones, especially during the time of eating, it is best to keep the phones away. Reunite the family back as it used to be.

After performing the prayers, forget about the phone as well until we recite the Qur'an. I mentioned in the previous chapter that during the time of *Adhan*, we should close the Qur'an if it is being recited and instead answer the call of prayers and repeat after the *mu'adhdhin*. However, I did not say not to read the Qur'an and scroll through our social media. I said to close the Qur'an—fold the Qur'an—so that later we will open it back and continue reciting it. When? After we have done the following: Repeat after the *Adhan*, make *wuḍu'* and read the *du'a'* for *wuḍu'* and pray the obligatory and supplementary prayers.

All these acts and supplications that I have mentioned are quite simple. Once we get used to them, they will, *inshā'Allāh,* not only give us access to enter *Jannah,* but also allow us to be invited to enter *Jannah* by whichever gate we want.

The key to *Jannah* is *ṣalah* and the key to *ṣalah* is *wuḍu*ʾ

CHAPTER 22

Du'a' to Be Firm on the *Deen*

We should always be grateful to Allah (s.w.t.) for guiding us to the straight path, for guiding us to Islam, and for inviting us to hear and read the knowledge of the *deen*. We should always utter "*Alḥamdulillāh*" for all the blessings that we have received and not take them for granted.

Unfortunately, there were some people around the Prophet (s.a.w.) who converted to disbelief after declaring Islam. Sadly, this still happens now. We would see some people who were very righteous at first, but then later they go astray.

That is why the most frequent *du'a'* of Prophet Muḥammad (s.a.w.) was:

يَا مُقَلِّبَ الْقُلُوبِ ثَبِّتْ قَلْبِي عَلَى دِينِكَ

Yā Muqallibal-qulūb, thabbit qalbī 'alā dīnik

"O' Allah, O' Overturner of hearts, make my heart firm in Your *deen*."

(Al-Adab Al-Mufrad 683)

Umm Salamah also mentioned in the hadith below that the supplication above was the one the Prophet (s.a.w.) did frequently:

Shahr bin Ḥawshab said:

I said to Umm Salamah: "O' Mother of the Believers! What was the supplication that the Messenger of Allah (s.a.w.) said most frequently when he was with you?" She said: "The supplication he said most frequently was: 'O' Changer of the hearts, make my heart firm upon Your religion (*Yā Muqallibal-qulūb, thabbit qalbī 'alā dīnik)*.'" She said: "So I said: 'O' Messenger of Allah, why do you supplicate so frequently: O' Changer of the hearts, make my heart firm upon Your religion?' He said: 'O' Umm Salamah! Verily, there is no human being except that his heart is between Two Fingers of the Fingers of Allah, so whomsoever He wills He makes steadfast, and whomever He wills He causes to deviate.'"

(Jamiʿ at-Tirmidhi 3522)

We too, should do the same and follow in the footsteps of our beloved Prophet (s.a.w.) and ask Allah to keep our hearts firm on this beautiful and peaceful religion.

What is something similar that we recite every day? What is the *du'a'* we say every day to ask Allah to keep us on His path? Even if we do not pray the sunnah prayers, we say this almost seventeen times in a day after praising and glorifying Allah the Almighty in our salah. It is "*Ihdinaṣ-ṣirāṭal-mustaqīm*"

ٱهْدِنَا ٱلصِّرَٰطَ ٱلْمُسْتَقِيمَ ٦

Guide us to the straight path.

(Qur'an, al-Fatiḥaḥ, 1:6)

O' Allah, guide us to the straight path.

O' Allah, keep us rightly guided on the straight path.

O'Allah, the One who changes our hearts, keep our hearts firm on Your religion.

Remember this, dear brothers and sisters: We only do good deeds because Allah (s.w.t) inspires us to do so. We only abstain from evil because Allah happens to ward us off from it and keep us away from evil deeds. And we will only enter *Jannah* through His mercy. And so, we should do as the Prophet (s.a.w.) taught us. We should follow in his footsteps, and we should make *du'a'* to enter *Jannah,* which I will mention in the next chapter.

To Allah alone we worship, and to Allah alone we ask for help.

Allah is the one who guides whomever He wills to His light.

CHAPTER 23

Du'a' for Jannah

The following is one of the *du'a's* that Prophet Muḥammad (s.a.w.) has taught us. The Prophet (s.a.w.) taught this supplication to 'A'ishah (r.a.) when she finished praying and told her (r.a.) to make this comprehensive supplication:

اللَّهُمَّ إِنِّي أَسْأَلُكَ مِنَ الْخَيْرِ كُلِّهِ عَاجِلِهِ
وَآجِلِهِ مَا عَلِمْتُ مِنْهُ وَمَا لَمْ أَعْلَمْ
وَأَعُوذُ بِكَ مِنَ الشَّرِّ كُلِّهِ عَاجِلِهِ وَآجِلِهِ
مَا عَلِمْتُ مِنْهُ وَمَا لَمْ أَعْلَمْ اللَّهُمَّ
إِنِّي أَسْأَلُكَ مِنْ خَيْرِ مَا سَأَلَكَ عَبْدُكَ

وَنَبِيُّكَ وَأَعُوذُ بِكَ مِنْ شَرِّ مَا عَاذَ بِهِ
عَبْدُكَ وَنَبِيُّكَ اللَّهُمَّ إِنِّي أَسْأَلُكَ الْجَنَّةَ
وَمَا قَرَّبَ إِلَيْهَا مِنْ قَوْلٍ أَوْ عَمَلٍ وَأَعُوذُ
بِكَ مِنَ النَّارِ وَمَا قَرَّبَ إِلَيْهَا مِنْ قَوْلٍ
أَوْ عَمَلٍ وَأَسْأَلُكَ أَنْ تَجْعَلَ كُلَّ قَضَاءٍ
قَضَيْتَهُ لِي خَيْرًا

Allāhumma ʾinnī ʾasʾaluka minal-khayri kullihi, ʿājilihi wa ʾājilihi, mā ʿalimtu minhu wa mā lam ʾaʿlam. Wa ʾaʿūdhu bika minnash-sharri kullihi, ʿājilihi wa ʾājilihi, mā ʿalimtu minhu wa mā lam ʾaʿlam. Allāhumma ʾinnī ʾasʾaluka min khayri mā saʿalaka ʿabduka wa nabiyyuka wa ʾaʿūdhu bika min sharri mā ʿādha bihi ʿabduka wa nabiyyuka. Allāhumma innī ʾasʾalukal-jannata wa mā qarraba ʾilayhā min qawlin ʾaw ʿamalin, wa ʾaʿūdhu bika minan-nāri wa mā qarraba ʾilayhā min qawlin ʾaw ʿamalin. Wa ʾasʾaluka ʾan tajʿala kulla qaḍāin qaḍaytahu lī khayran.

"O' Allah, I ask You for all that is good in this world and in the Hereafter, what I know and what I do not know. O' Allah, I seek refuge with You from all evil, in this world and in

> the Hereafter, what I know and what I do not know. O' Allah, I ask You for the good that Your slave and Prophet has asked You for, and I seek refuge with You from the evil from which Your slave and Prophet sought refuge. O' Allah, I ask You for Paradise and for that which brings one closer to it, in word and deed, and I seek refuge in You from Hell and from that which brings one closer to it, in word and deed. And I ask You to make every decree that You decree concerning me good."
>
> (Sunan ibn Majah 3846)

In essence, dear brothers and sisters, memorise it and recite it.

Jannah is worth it.

Jannah is where we will attain **comfort**.

Jannah is where we will be **free** from any **pain** and **hatred**.

Jannah is where we will be **reunited** with our **loved ones**.

Jannah is where we will attain **eternal peace**.

Jannah is where we will attain **everlasting happiness**.

So, race towards the **forgiveness** and **mercy** of **Allah** the Almighty to attain this **gift**.

Ending Remarks

Dear brothers and sisters, I hope that *inshā'Allāh*, one day, we will all be sitting in *Jannatul-Firdaws* together whilst remembering this lecture and this book. It is an exceptionally beautiful thing to always read on the knowledge of Allah and attend lectures and classes as well.

One of my favourite hadiths is in which the Prophet (s.a.w.) mentioned that Allah has created angels whose duty is to travel across the world to find people who are gathered for the *deen*—for learning the knowledge of the *deen* or for praising Allah.

The angels will descend to these gatherings and will call on one another, saying, "Come, come. There is a *ḥalaqah*. There is a gathering of people reciting the *dhikr*." Afterwards, the angels will ascend to Allah (s.w.t.) to report to him. Allah knows best, and He will still ask the angels, "How did you find My servants?" The angels will say, "We found them praising and invoking you."

Abu Hurayrah and Abu Sa'id Al-Khudri (r.a.) reported:

> "The Messenger of Allah (s.a.w.) said, 'When a group of people assemble for the remembrance of Allah, the angels surround them (with their wings), (Allah's) mercy envelops them, *sakinah* or tranquillity descends upon them, and Allah makes a mention of them before those who are near Him.'"
>
> (Riyaḍ aṣ-Ṣaliḥin 1448)

Allah will then ask, "What did they say?" The angels will say, "They supplicated, 'O' Allah, we ask of You for Heaven, and we seek refuge with You against Hellfire.'" Allah will then ask the angels, and He knows best, "Have they seen My Heaven? Have they seen My Hellfire?" The angels will answer, "Of course not." Then He (s.w.t.) will ask, "What if they see them?" The angels will say, "Then they will be keener on asking for Heaven and seeking refuge from Hellfire." Allah will then say to the angels, "Bear witness, I have answered their *du'a'*, and I have granted them Heaven, and I have protected them against Hellfire."

Some of the angels will then say, "O'Allah, so-and-so did not come to the gathering because they wanted to. They came for another reason pertaining to *dunya*. What about them?" Allah will say, "Anyone who happens to be among them shall receive the same reward, shall receive salvation and enter Heaven and be protected from Hellfire because of the beautiful company."

Simply because of the beautiful company that we are surrounded with, Allah will grant us the same reward—salvation, the reward to be eligible to enter *Jannah* and be protected from Hellfire.

We have been talking about Allah (s.w.t.), praising Him (s.w.t.), reciting His words, learning His knowledge, learning the sunnah of His Messenger (s.a.w.), invoking Him and asking for His salvation. Everyone who attends *ḥalaqah* will not be ruined. Everyone who tries to learn more about the *deen* of Allah will not be ruined, *inshā'Allāh.* May Allah pardon us and forgive us for all of our sins. May Allah grant us *Jannatul-Firdaws*.

Whoever follows a path in the pursuit of knowledge of the *deen*,

Allah will make the path to *Jannah* easy for them.

Arabic Glossary

Adhan - The call to prayer

ʿAbdi - Servant

Alḥamdulillāh - Praise be to Allah

Al-Isra'wal Miʿraj - The two parts of the night journey and ascension of the Prophet Muḥammad (s.a.w.) from Makkah to Masjid al-Aqṣa and from Masjid al-Aqṣa to the Heavens

An-Naar - Hellfire

ʿArsh - The Throne of Allah

Ash-shahawat - The things we desire

Astagfirullāh - I seek forgiveness in Allah

Ayyam al-Biḍ - The White Days. These are the 13th, 14th, and 15th days of each lunar month.

Bisharah - Good news/Glad tidings

Daʿwah - A call to embrace Islam

Deen - Religion

Dhikr - Remembrance to Allah

Ḍuḥa - Morning supplementary prayer

Dunya - Worldly life

Fawaḥish - Shameful deeds and immoralities

Fitnah - The test and trials of life

Ḥajj - Pilgrimage

Ḥalaqah - A religious gathering or an Islamic study circle

Ḥusnul khatimah - Good ending of life

Iman - Faith

Inshā'Allāh - If Allah wills

Jahannam - Hellfire

Jannah - Heaven

Jannatul-Firdaws - Gardens of *Firdaws* (the highest place in Heaven)

Jihad - The struggle or strive against injustice, barriers and odds

Khamr - Intoxicants/Wine

Makruh - Disliked

Mashā'Allāh - As Allah has willed

Mujahidin - People who engage in *Jihad*

Mu'adhdhin - The person who gives the call of *Adhan*

Ṣadaqah - Charity

Sakinah - Tranquillity

Ṣalah - Prayer

Shafa'ah - Intercession

Sirah - The biography or life story of a person

Ṣirat - The straight path/the bridge every person will cross on the Day of Judgement.

SubḥānAllāh - Glory be to Allah

Sujud - Prostration

Tahajjud - Night prayer

Ummah - Muslim community

Wajib - Obligatory act

Wuḍu' - Ablution

Zakah - Almsgiving

www.ingramcontent.com/pod-product-compliance
Lightning Source LLC
LaVergne TN
LVHW061615070526
838199LV00078B/7296
* 9 7 8 9 6 7 2 8 4 4 4 0 2 *